"Easier to read than David Brooks or Bill Bryson, this accessible book fills a niche between popular culture and the academic world. Call this sociology light with a comic twist."

— Eric Roth, author of *Compelling Conversations*

"This book presents an insightful look into the hearts and minds of Americans. It also explains the nuances of American culture that would take one years to figure out for oneself."

— Dr. Ashay Dhamdhere

"What other book has illustrations and statistics to show common American attitudes and behavior? This book is truly unique. The author objectively describes the controversial issues affecting Americans, such as multiple identities, non-traditional families, and feelings of patriotism. It is the funniest, clearest, and the truest picture of American culture today."

— Livia Tommasini, Italian biotech researcher

"If you have come to the U.S. to visit or stay, and you don't want to feel just like another tourist, this book is exactly what you need."

— Bent Soelberg, Manager, Business School of Southern Denmark

"If you are only going to read one book about Americans, you must read this one."

— Walt Lee, Chinese director of Futurewei Technologies

"'What is America?' Everyone has a different answer to this question, and yet few have thought as deeply or creatively as Diane Asitimbay. She provides a witty and insightful guidebook for understanding that elusive phenomenon, "America," a country born of a democratic idea, inhabited by people from all other nations, and educated by an entertainment industry."

— Robert A. Pastor, Professor of International Affairs,
American University

What's Up, America?
A Foreigner's Guide to Understanding Americans

Diane Asitimbay

Culturelink Press
San Diego, CA

Culturelink Press, P.O. Box 3538, San Diego, CA 92163

What's Up, America? Second Edition

PRINTED IN THE UNITED STATES OF AMERICA

Library of Congress Cataloging-in-Publication Data

Asitimbay, Diane.
    What's Up, America? : a foreigner's guide to
understanding Americans / Diane Asitimbay.
        p. cm.
    Includes bibliographical references and index.
    ISBN-10: 0-9759276-3-9
    ISBN-13: 978-0-9759276-3-2

Previously catalogued as:
1. United States--Handbooks, manuals, etc. 2. United
States--Social life and customs--1971---Handbooks,
manuals, etc. 3. Visitors, Foreign--United States--
Handbooks, manuals, etc.   I. Title.

E158.A84 2004   973   2004096796

For Institutional and Quantity Orders:
Culturelink Press
P.O. Box 3538
San Diego, CA 92163
Tel. (619) 501-9873

Cover illustration by Jim Whiting
Cover design and composition by Kirsten Chandler

Visit our website at: www.culturelinkpress.com

Acknowledgments

I would like to thank my husband Angel and my daughter Sonia for lending their enduring patience and support while writing this book. A special thanks to Gyanam Sadananda, a dear friend who critiqued my book and encouraged me at the same time. I am indebted to Lindy Ferguson for her editing of my early draft and for giving me practical advice. A big thanks to George Simons who gave his valuable feedback on this second edition. And finally, to all the international students that have come into my life, for inspiring me to write this book, thank you.

Contents

Introduction

U nlike other books that will tell you what American culture is, *What's Up, America?* tackles the why questions foreigners ask Americans and no one wants to answer. This book explains the values behind what Americans do. In doing so, it uncovers the hidden rules of the culture and for the first time, reveals the American psyche to foreigners.

Since the first edition of *What's Up, America?* was published, this book has taken on a life of its own. It has been used in a variety of courses including classes of English language study, American studies, student exchange programs, orientation programs for international students and introductory college courses in cultural anthropology and sociology.

Readers will find this second edition expanded with new chapters on the American health care system and U.S. sports. People who have come from countries that have national health insurance have asked me how the largely private U.S. health care system works. I hope their questions have been answered in the new chapter entitled "Ills, Pills, and Medical Bills." The sports chapter was also the product of many conversations with international visitors about sports. Newcomers scratch their heads and ask, "How come Americans have so much passion for their four professional sports other than the world's beloved "football?" This has led me to write the new sports chapter called, "A Game for All Seasons." Finally, I have updated the statistics for this second edition based on new reports and surveys whenever it was possible.

What's Up, America? sets out to take the image of Americans out of the television tube and makes them into real live three-dimensional people, with their myths, paradoxes and prejudices. By examining twenty-two aspects of the American character and lifestyle, it unlocks the secrets of how Americans really live. It will take the international visitor inside the culture to reveal American passions and obsessions up close, where the landscape is often different from what was expected.

While I was writing this book, I realized the risks. We all know Americans come in all shapes and sizes, as do our mindsets and beliefs. Because of our differences, some Americans believe that it is impossible to generalize about American culture without turning to stereotypes. While I realize there are variations on what I have written about American culture, I do believe there are distinguishing cultural patterns that identify American behavior. Though I have made judgments about my culture and people throughout the book, I have often shown the cultural habits of not only the mainstream culture, but also the ethnic subcultures. I have also taken into account some of the regional differences in the United States.

Though *What's Up, America?* aims to reduce the culture shock that foreigners face, it is also for Americans who want to broaden their world view. The book compares American cultural habits to other parts of the world. This offers a unique global perspective to American readers. If Americans become more curious about people from other countries and learn something about their cultural habits, it will improve our friendships and business relationships with our global partners.

Since the Internet and cell phone have shrunk the world into a size that everyone is talking about, I believe the international perspective in *What's Up, America?* makes this book unlike any other handbook.

These international comparisons are based on my travels and work abroad as a journalist as well as the numerous discussions with international students inside and outside the classroom. The book is also supported by research, ranging from up-to-date U.S. Census reports to current surveys cited at the end of the book. Though the Census is taken every ten years in the United States, I have included government updates whenever they were available. Every effort has been made to make this book as complete and as accurate as possible. Graphs throughout the book illustrate facts and figures about Americans, which I hope readers will find useful.

From candid reflections on the American family, to detailed explanations of the American mindset, this book can be referred to when you have questions about the American landscape and people. It is my hope that these insights into the American character will help those who visit or live in the United States have a more valuable experience. *What's Up, America?* can serve as an indispensable tool for Americans who have traveled abroad, plan a trip, or who have contact with international people.

Think of it as a road trip, with every chapter a place to stop and look around at the American landscape. Wherever you are in the journey of your American experience, I would love to hear from you. Please don't hesitate to contact me with your suggestions and comments. You can e-mail me at www.culturelinkpress.com or write me c/o Culturelink Press, P.O. Box 3538, San Diego, CA 92163. Your feedback will contribute valuable information that I will pass on to others through revisions of this book.

Growing Up

16 yrs. old – Getting a driver's license is a rite of passage in the United States.

18 yrs. old – You are an adult by law. You can vote, serve in the military, and marry without your parent's permission.

21 yrs. old – You can drink alcohol.

25-34 yrs. old – You usually live on your own. Only 22% of young Americans, ages 25-34, live at home.

Growing Old

Retirement: 65 yrs. old – About 12.4% or one in every eight Americans is a senior.

75 yrs. or older – Half of women age 75 or older live alone, usually because their spouses have died.

85 yrs. or older – Few seniors live in nursing homes, but after the age of 85, the number of seniors who live in this kind of housing sharply rises to 19%.

Source: National Center for Health Statistics & The U.S. Census Bureau

Chapter 1:

Growing Up & Growing Old

When you grow up in the United States, *you*, the individual, are valued more than the family as a whole. Some people call this concept independence; others call it self-centeredness. The notion of individual needs coming before the needs of others is taught before you can even talk. Your mother says, "That's *your* cup, that's *your* spoon, that's *your* chair." The process of mentally stamping objects with your name begins. If a family member or a visitor wants to use whatever is stamped yours, they must ask your permission, even if they are children and you are an adult.

You choose. This is what you hear, like an echo, from every corner of the United States. It begins at an early age. You are faced with several choices throughout the day, that add up to thousands of choices in a lifetime. Parents constantly ask their children what they want. For example, a little boy of around four years old steps into an ice cream shop with his mother. "Andrew," the mom says, "would you like vanilla, chocolate, chocolate chip, caramel, or strawberry?" Before the child understands yet alone remembers his choices, the mom continues, "They have nuts, M&Ms and sprinkles. Would you like a topping on your ice cream or just plain? The kid remains silent and looks confused. The mom, frustrated and impatient, raises her voice at the child: "Andrew, answer me!"

"I want uh . . . Uh . . ." The child tries to decide.

The mom gives up and quickly turns to the clerk to say, "He'll have a vanilla cone with sprinkles on it." This is how the seed of independence is planted in a culture where we are called upon to make up our own minds rather than allow parents to make decisions for us, and this is why some cultures think of us as a child-oriented society.

What if a child misbehaves? Americans punish their children by taking away privileges like watching TV or playing video games. Some parents send their misbehaving children to their bedroom. But today, American children have so many entertaining toys and gadgets in their bedroom that this kind of punishment isn't as effective as in the past. At least in the eyes of some people, it isn't considered punishment anymore.

Another form of social isolation is the time-out chair. Children must sit in a chair and be completely silent until parents decide their children have been properly punished according to their misbehavior. How long they must stay in this punishment chair depends on some basic ideas about punishment in America. Children must admit to the parent what they have done wrong, apologize to the parent and promise not to do it again. This is what we call the making-up process.

Grounding, or not being able to go outside with your friends, is another typical punishment. Some parents spank their children when they are young, but after the children get older, parents usually stop. In the United States, schools and courts publicly watch parents closely if parents hit their children. Children are aware of this at an early age because our schools educate them about child abuse. There are even billboards on the roadside advertising a toll-free hotline where children can report their parents for child abuse.

Chores and Allowance

Chores usually begin at about five years old. Young children typically clean their rooms and set or clear away the table. As we get older, we begin to do the dishes, take out the garbage and mow the lawn. Parents view these jobs as necessary for children to learn how to take care of themselves. Some families give money or an allowance to their children for doing chores.

The allowance given to children in the United States, though many parents deny it, is often tied to the work the child does for the parents. If you don't do your chores, you usually don't get an allowance. It is understood that children can spend the money they earned from chores on whatever they want.

Critics believe this practice teaches children to be motivated by monetary awards rather than family responsibility. This attitude of "What do I get in return?" is reflected in the dynamics of the family. Many children fail to help family members voluntarily without some concrete, often financial, award being established beforehand. While American parents argue that this practice builds money management skills and the work ethic, it could be argued that children are becoming the newest members of the economy by spending their allowances.

Becoming Independent

American children gradually become used to being physically separated from their parents. It doesn't happen overnight. First, working parents leave their children with babysitters, and at daycare centers where child-care workers take care of them rather than family members. As many families have neighbors without children, parents must make play dates. These are scheduled times when their children play with their friends, and parents often coordinate drop-off and pick-up times with business-like precision.

Then, when a child reaches six or seven years of age, they usually begin to have sleepovers. A child spends the night at a friend's house where they get to watch videos together and eat pizza. Young children are away from their parents at night for the first time. In summer, when school is out, children often go away to day camps like the YMCA or even live at the camps for the entire summer.

By the time American young people reach 16, the age to legally work in this country, they have already spent a great deal of time away from their parents. They have already had experience earning their own money by doing chores at home or neighborhood jobs such as babysitting and mowing the lawn. Teenagers then work part time for "real pay" at a fast-food restaurant. They start to buy their own clothes and CDs and go to the movies with the money they have earned.

There are really two-and-a-half steps to adulthood in the United States: at ages 16, 18 and 21. The first important step happens at 16 years old when you begin to drive. Getting a driver's license in the United States is your passage into adulthood. Your mother no longer has to drop you off and pick you up for your baseball game or dance practice anymore. You can go out alone at night with your friends, and the variety and kinds of activities you can do in your car are endless.

American parents know the dangers and risks of driving and worry, but they allow their children this independence anyway. They weigh the risks against their own needs. Working parents value the teenager who can help them run an errand with the car, from grocery shopping to dropping off film to be developed. The car, and the mobility it provides for the teenager, is the first break with the family, and it is a very personal one.

At this time, parents begin to set curfews as to when the teenager must be home. In many cities across the United States, cities have imposed curfews too. Young people under the age of 18 must be off the streets by 11 p.m. during the week and midnight on weekends. Teens who are going to or from a night job are exempt from the law, as are teens traveling with parents. Curfew laws began as a way to reduce violence, but most young people believe these government rules are unfair.

The second step to adulthood is when you are 18. You become psychologically and legally independent from your parents. You can vote and go into the military, and people can take you to court and sue you instead of your parents. American parents tend to think that now that you are legally and financially responsible for yourself, they can breathe a sigh of relief when you go out with friends. Even if the financial dependence on your parents continues, the psychological and legal independence is clear. Teenagers 18 or older have the attitude of "I can do what I want now that I'm an adult."

Achieving full financial independence from your parents usually occurs after graduating from high school or college. Young people are split into two groups when they graduate from high school: those who look for a full-time job and those who go to college. Whatever path the high school graduate takes, the young person usually lives away from home for the first time.

Knowing this day of final separation will come, parents often remind their children of the future need "to make it on their own." Teenagers already have this in the back of their minds and try to separate themselves emotionally and psychologically from their parents too. From an early age, many smaller steps have been taken to be able to make the final break at 18. Breaking the emotional connection to Mom and Dad is reflected in our language with idiomatic expressions such as "make the break from your parents" or "cut the apron strings."

Parents view severing emotional ties with their children or "letting their children go" as a sign of love. They see it as the ultimate self-sacrifice of suppressing their will and allowing their children to make their own way in life. As their child nears 18 years old, the parents' influence gradually diminishes. Important decisions made by the 18-year-old vary, but might include selecting the college they want to go to, choosing a major or field of study, and leading the kind of lifestyle they want, with friends they desire. The parents' diminished role in their children's life is more or less difficult for many parents to accept.

The last step to full legal independence is at 21, when you are allowed to drink alcohol in the United States. This is a minor step, though, as most teenagers have already tried drinking with their friends or may drink secretly at parties. It is now only a matter of making the fact public and being able to go to bars.

By the age of 21 or 22, many young people want to move to a different city or state from where their parents live. This geographic separation is symbolic of the psychological and emotional distance. While adult children are working or going to college, getting married and having kids, their parents are growing old, so mothers and fathers turn into grandparents who live far from not only their children but also their grandchildren.

Adult children differ on how much contact they maintain with their parents when they live out of state or in a different city. If they live out of state, some adult children call their parents every week, others every month or even only once or twice a year. It is common to "visit the folks," as parents are commonly called, when we take a summer vacation or a major holiday such as Thanksgiving, Christmas, or Easter.

Some families, especially immigrant families who grow up in a subculture, do not follow this pattern of independence. Parents of Mexican Americans or Asian

Americans often play an active role in their adult children's lives beyond 18 years old.

This family separation differs from many countries in the world. In Italy and Southern Europe, young people often live with their parents into their late 20s or 30's, or until they get married. In Arab countries, families have their relatives live in the neighborhood, sometimes within the same block. They frequently live with an extended family. In Japan, because children study all day, maintaining a close relationship to their dads is particularly difficult. Japanese fathers often are away from their homes more hours than their American counterparts. They frequently dine with colleagues after work besides the long hours spent working at their jobs. Some Japanese dads might even work in another city, and visit their families on weekends. Yet when it comes time to marrying and establishing households, Japanese married couples usually live close to their families. In Korea, it is still common for a married couple to live with the husband's parents and to take care of them as they age.

Growing Old

While their children are growing up, parents are growing old. Then they turn 65, retire, and become senior citizens. Now they have a lot of free time on their hands. In the United States, seniors play golf and bingo, take classes, gamble and travel to other countries. Generally, they fill their free time with many activities they were unable to pursue when working.

American seniors cherish this "individual pursuit of happiness." As parents, they are eager to let their children leave home at 18. For twenty years, they haven't had any children living with them. When grandchildren finally come along, some active seniors choose not to take care of them. That responsibility would hinder them from pursuing their self-fulfilling activities. Others would rather not be around the noise and activity that young children bring.

The paradox of this self-centered lifestyle is that many of these same seniors volunteer many hours at museums, churches, historical societies, and other civic organizations. They even volunteer at youth organizations and schools where they take care of children many hours a week. Yet many seniors who are grandparents may spend little time with their own grandchildren.

Life may turn upside down, though, for both the adult children and the aging parent, in a single moment if a senior parent has a heart attack or is diagnosed with a serious medical condition.

The whole issue of independence that was settled once and for all after high school or college comes back again. But this time, the process is reversed. Parents are struggling to maintain their independence from their adult children.

But for many families, the circle has been broken. Over the course of twenty to thirty years, day-to-day life for both the parents and the adult children has become a mystery. Emotional distance has been established in the years of long-distance, routine phone calls. Adult children may look at the sickly parent as an inconvenience rather than feel the passionate need to take care of them.

The reality is that many adult children do not want their parents to live with them. Many adult children are not ready to make sacrifices for their aging parents. These sacrifices may include taking time off from their jobs, or reducing their hours if both husband and wife hold down jobs. In short, they are not willing to change their lifestyle in that way.

On the other hand, older people try not to depend on their adult children. They feel guilty for needing their children. Our culture admires the strong and teaches us not to show our weak side. If you ask senior citizens why they don't live with their children, you will most likely hear, "I don't want to be a burden to my children."

What does being a burden mean to them? If you press a senior into answering, it usually revolves around being forced to ask their adult children to do simple errands for them.

Being able to drive yourself where you want to go when you're old is very important. Driving is symbolic of independence in American culture. Remember when you were 16 years old and this was the rite of passage? Seniors also cherish their driver's license and are reluctant to give it up no matter how bad their eyesight is or how much medication they are taking. They feel it is a sign of defeat in the battle to stay independent.

The pressure of not living with your parents after 18 is just as strong as not living with your children when you are 80.

That's why there are many kinds of living arrangements for seniors. There are senior complexes, assisted living complexes, basic nursing homes, skilled nursing homes, and a myriad of other kinds of housing for seniors today. Many foreigners mistakenly believe most Americans put their parents in nursing homes. Actually, only 4% of seniors 65 to 85 years of age live in nursing homes in the United States according to the National Center for Health Statistics. Most seniors live alone or with their husband or wife. For seniors over 85 years old, however, the numbers dramatically increase to 19%. By this age, many seniors have become widowed and have more serious medical conditions.

A few seniors realize that no one will take care of them if they get sick and live far from their children. They get frightened at the thought of being sick and alone before any major medical problems occur. Some seniors might even get frightened enough to sell their home and move close to where their children are.

It is a myth that the American government takes the place of the family institution and financially supports the elderly in the United States. When you turn 65 and retire, you get two things to help you live on a very reduced income. You get free medical insurance called Medicare, which many doctors do not accept, as they are only minimally reimbursed. And you may get a pension or a social security check.

Not everyone gets social security in the United States when they turn 65, either. Only people who have worked a certain number of years, which amounts to about 10 years of full-time work, receive a regular check. Or when your spouse dies, you may collect a major portion of his or her social security check.

The average senior income from social security is $14,000 a year. This is next to impossible to live on unless you have no house payment. This is why seniors have so many discounts in our society, ranging from reduced prices on entertainment, senior days in stores, and a special rate for bus passes.

Prescription drugs are expensive in the United States, and many of these drugs are not covered by this government insurance. This forces seniors to buy their medicines in cheaper places like Canada and Mexico.

Who will take care of us when we are old? *Nobody* has been the answer so far in our culture. Seniors make up 12% of American society today, and this age group is the fastest growing segment of our population. As we live longer and have fewer children, the need for adult children to take care of their aging parents will become greater. Will it be great enough to change our youth-centered culture?

Notes

"In America, the young are always ready to give those who are older than themselves the full benefits of their inexperience."

– Oscar Wilde, humorist (1856-1900)

Don't Worry, Be Happy.

The yellow smiley face is a universal symbol of good cheer. This cultural icon was created by Harvey Ball in 1963 as part of a campaign to improve employee morale at an insurance company.

Have a Nice Day! is one of the most overused expressions in the United States. Since the 1970's, it has been used to end a conversation in place of the traditional "goodbye."

Does this goodbye phrase truly cheer someone up or does it force people to hide how they really feel? Customer service people are often expected to use this phrase to show enthusiasm to customers.

Sweden or Switzerland?

○ Americans age 18 to 24 came in next to last among nine countries in the National Geographic and Roper 2002 Survey, a survey which measured students' knowledge of geography.

○ On this geographic survey, more than half, 56%, of Americans could not locate India, home to 17% of the world's population.

Chapter 2:

Thinking American

W hy are Americans always smiling? We are walking "smiley signs" ending our conversations with, "Have a nice day." Those happy words seem to slip from our tongues without any real thought. "Don't worry, be happy." There are smiley face stickers and icons, and there is even a huge smiley face structure off Interstate 80, "Smiley, the Friendly Greeter," a city landmark for a small town in Illinois.

Customer service in stores is built on a grin. At the checkout counter, cashiers greet you with a rehearsed happy face and ask, "Was everything okay?" or "Did you find everything you needed?"

What enormous pressure we have in this culture to at least *look* happy. If you appear too serious, people will chide you by saying, "Don't look so serious." Or they might ask you, "Is something wrong?" It's common to hear, "Yes, I'm having a bad day." Then the person typically replies, "Oh, I'm sorry to hear that," or "That's too bad." This is a ritual that usually doesn't go further than a polite exchange of unhappiness and sympathy.

This need to be eternally pleasant seems to be a contradiction in the United States, where the freedom to speak up and say what you feel is honestly valued. Public discourse in the form of debates before a presidential campaign is common. You can protest in front of a business or government organization, expressing your personal opinion in a public place. Yet at the same time, there is an unwritten cultural rule that many Americans learn from an early age. Parents usually teach their children to be polite and not offend anyone. If the topic is negative or if children want to criticize someone, they should keep their opinions to themselves. We are taught to talk only about pleasant subjects. This is why we may appear so superficial and, when taken to the extreme, not honest about the way we feel towards someone. We aren't supposed to talk about religion, politics, and sex because it might make other people feel uncomfortable.

We have happy hours at bars and restaurants, when cheaper drinks are offered so you can drink more and be happier. McDonald's sells us not a children's hamburger but a "Happy Meal." Your bank and dentist send you cards wishing you a happy birthday.

Happiness is commercialized and packaged to be bought and sold. The deep realities of human existence, such as sickness, old age and death, are not discussed. We avoid coming face to face with these aspects of life, yet we expect to have a rich, emotional connection to people.

We sell happiness in a bottle. Anti-depressants are the most frequently prescribed drugs in the U.S., reports the Center for Disease Control in 2007. It seems the difference between treating sadness and clinical disease is less clear today.

Our movies usually end happily. They send out a distorted vision of real life in our society but reveal how Americans want their lives to be. *Pretty Woman* and *Maid in Manhattan* are Cinderella stories of today. Children are first raised on fairy tales where the prince finds the slipper of his princess and lives happily ever after. The poor girl marries the rich man and lives in bliss. Or in action movies, the hero is shot at numerous times, surviving bullets and car crashes, but he never dies. Adult fairy tales are very popular in movies because we search for that version of happiness.

Happiness is featured in television sitcoms like *Jerry Seinfeld* and *Friends*, which usually create one-liner jokes every few seconds and expect you to laugh with the prerecorded laughter. The one-liner is the classic American brand of humor. It is basically a put down or an insult said in a joking way, so that you laugh at yourself rather than feel offended or hurt.

Whether we like you or not, the American style of conversing is mainly through jokes. Most Americans have a very direct sense of humor compared to the sophisticated British wit. Ethnic jokes were commonly told in the past but today, jokes are mostly told about gender, weakness of character, and we have plenty of lawyer jokes too.

Many Americans are thought to be gullible. We readily trust in people's words without analyzing or judging the source. "You have my word," we say. By looking at people in the eye, we judge whether they are telling the truth or not.

Geographically Illiterate

Many Americans are geographically illiterate. We don't know Switzerland from Sweden. We're not sure if people in Brazil speak Spanish or Portuguese. In a recent geography poll, more than 3,000 young people (18-24 year olds) were surveyed in nine countries about their knowledge of geography. Overall, Sweden scored the highest and the United States was next to last. About 11 percent of young Americans couldn't even locate the United States on an unlabeled world map, 29 percent couldn't locate the Pacific Ocean, 58 percent didn't know where France was, and 69 percent couldn't find the United Kingdom.

The paradox of living in a country that is a leader in global politics, yet has the majority of people ignorant about the rest of the world, is a fact of American culture. Young people know more about the South Pacific island featured on the TV show *Survivor* than where Iraq and Israel are.

Geography is usually not required in American schools and is instead, offered as an elective. Students may avoid taking a class because it's not a subject on our standardized tests. Schools focus on preparing students in core subjects that they will later be tested on: mathematics, science, and English. In elementary school, Americans study their native state for one whole school year by learning the state's flower, resources, motto, and history as part of the subject of social science. Then we briefly study geography again in high school in our American History and World History classes, whose main focus is a history of wars and heroes. It is puzzling to think that students could learn history without basic geography skills.

Only 20% of Americans have traveled or studied abroad in any given year. Although traveling to another country surely would help shed some of the geographic ignorance, most Americans grow up visiting sites within the United States. It is common to go to other states to visit relatives or to go camping in national parks. Families often drive to these places, and see their vacation as a chance to get away from the city.

Taking the whole family to another country for vacation is quite unusual as well as expensive. The American concept for vacation is often anti-urban as well. Going to the countryside or beach to absorb the natural environment and get away from traffic is often sought rather than seeing a large city in another country and exploring its cultural wealth.

Another explanation for our ignorance of other countries is that the vast majority of Americans, about 85%, speak only one language. When Americans do travel abroad, they don't want to learn another language. Many are not forced to, as English is widely spoken in many of the European countries that Americans like to visit. Though American students are increasingly going to other countries such as Spain and Italy, the United Kingdom is still the leading destination for American students, according to a 2008 Open Doors report, an annual report that tracks college students who study overseas.

Still another part of our geographical illiteracy can be explained by our history. Early American colonists came here and settled down on unchartered territory. We were never forced to defend our land from foreign conquerors. To the east and the west, the United States has no border countries to contend with. The Pacific and the Atlantic oceans have protected and isolated us from other continents. This geographical inheritance has produced an American mindset that views foreigners as a labor force, and not as a cultural or language force.

Number Crazy

How much and how many are always on our minds. We rate every human experience and dissect it into numbers.

Listen to our traffic reports. We report on traffic as if it were a science with codes for highways and congestion: "Four lanes open on the eastbound 8 and a 25-minute wait off the 15-interchange where it merges with the 805, you have a 3-car pileup averaging a 45-minute delay on the 5. Stay tuned for updates every 15 minutes."

Weather reports are similar with sunshine measured by UV (ultraviolet) indexes and humidity and precipitation percentages. All this number jargon makes our head spin, when in reality, all we want to know is the temperature and whether it's going to rain or not.

Americans suffer from a disease that I call *"the -est"* problem. We are a nation of superlatives. Statistics published in newspapers or seen on TV often are selected to show the United States as the best in everything and the only important country.

You can really see *"the -est"* problem in our media. We publish lists of "the best" all the time. We quantify everything and then compare it to other countries and people. The fastest growing religion is Islam, the richest American is Bill Gates and the biggest hit in the movie theaters was *The Titanic. The New York Times* produces a bestseller list of books that is printed weekly in our newspapers. And of course, we love the ultimate -*est* book, the *Guinness Book of World Records*. Nothing in the United States can be just pleasant, good or fair. It must be super, fantastic, wonderful or awesome, the prettiest, the fastest, the highest and the best. If you talk about averages or the median, Americans will ask you for the minimum and maximum or the best and the worst. We are a nation of extremes. We think moderation is boring.

International news practically doesn't exist in the United States. Even *The New York Times*, one of the most respected newspapers in the country, devotes only a few pages to international news. Of course, if you have cable, there is always *CNN* and there is *BBC*, but many times the focus is just on crises and conflicts in political parts of the world that the United States is militarily involved in. When the World Cup was held in the United States in 1994, Americans who had no cable TV service had to watch the games in Spanish because the major network channels only televised games when the Americans played. We were hosting the World Cup and we only wanted to see our country's team play? This was more than just the lack of interest in soccer in the United States. It demonstrated that only "American" sports are considered important enough for prime time television.

A Television Mind

When I ask international students whom they admire most in their lives, they usually say their parents or grandparents. When I ask the same question to American students, most name a famous movie or TV star.

The average American has the TV set on for 7 hours and 40 minutes a day and watches over 4 hours of programs a day, reports Nielsen, a television ratings service. American children and teens have more media choices with the Internet but instead of spending less time watching TV, the amount of time watching TV has stayed the same. In other words, media use has simply increased. Besides all the TV-watching, American young people now spend an additional one and half hours listening to music and at least another hour using their computers to play games, chat on-line and do homework.

Besides the fact that the TV set is turned on several hours a day at home, the television screen is also turned on in public places. The TV is seen in health clubs, bars and restaurants and in doctors' and mechanics' waiting rooms. Even when we go to a baseball game where we are paying to see the action and players in person, people watch an enormous screen. Viewing is preferred to doing. The constant noise from the TV in public places offers very little silence for people to read and think. It may confirm the idea that Americans are not comfortable in silence.

In our homes too, many American parties are planned around watching television. You are invited to come to our house and watch the Super Bowl, the Rose Bowl, the Oscars, the Macy's Thanksgiving Parade, and the Times Square ball dropping on New Year's Eve. You sit in front of the television with other guests and exchange commentary about what you watch. Some people invite guests to their home and have the TV turned on in the background just in case they don't find enough to talk about.

Many Americans talk about TV programs as if the knowledge and adventures on TV were their own. Sharing first-hand experience is becoming rare, and TV programs often replace genuine topics of conversation. Seeing the world through a commercial box comes with a price, though. Commercials are constantly interrupting our programs asking us to buy this product or that, so our attention spans are split into tiny parts too.

Talking as a Game

Be prepared to play ping-pong when you talk to Americans. You say something brief, usually no more than one sentence. Then the other person asks a question. The other person answers it and says something short again. Your head bobs back and forth as you watch two Americans talk to each other.

Many aspects of our culture use sports and games as a metaphor. We use the notion of a ball in our daily speech and particularly in business. It's your turn to decide or act can be *the ball is in your court*. When you avoid responsibility *you drop the ball*. You *pitch an idea* means presenting a person with your idea, with the intention of convincing them of your plan. Have you done your job thoroughly? Then you've *covered all the bases*. You're a *big hitter, a major player*, meaning an important competitor in business.

We borrow words from many sports, but baseball, in particular is widely used. We present an idea or *throw out* an idea. We give you two chances in the *game of life* or business. With the third chance, you lose or face the consequences. It's *three strikes and you're out*.

We can also think of dating as a game, with baseball capturing the hearts of Americans. In a chauvinistic way, American males often use slang to express how far they physically advance with a woman on a date. When a male says he only got to *first base* this means he was only able to hold hands with the girl or give her a peck on the cheek. Getting to *second base* might mean he managed to kiss her, *third base* he made out with her or was able to touch her.

Finally, if he *hit a home run*, he managed to sleep with her. He *scored*! If he *struck out*, this means he was unsuccessful at advancing to any of these bases with the girl.

Lonely or Alone?

We often feel isolated and alone in the United States. One in every four Americans lives alone. We tell the most personal details of our lives to strangers in grocery lines, in restaurants, and to therapists, but not to people we know or family members. When Americans have a serious problem in a relationship, we run to the therapist. The pressure in our society to be self-reliant is so strong that we don't want to expose our weaknesses and be judged by our friends and family. We choose the stranger in seeking help to solve our problems. We also trust in their specialized knowledge more than our own family.

Dogmatic

Why are Americans so dogmatic? Americans like a yes or no when asked a question. We dislike ambiguity. We see reality in black and white photos rather than in color. Things that can't be researched to find facts and conclusions make us feel uneasy. Americans think in a linear, straight ahead method and don't like digressions.

When Americans fail to understand each other, we might say, "I don't understand your line of reasoning," or if we speak indirectly about a topic, we might urge the other person to "please get to the point." Americans often dislike uncertainty. When we ask you what you want to do or where you want to go, we usually feel frustrated with any hesitation or lengthy explanation. We might even ask you rather abruptly, *"Yes or No?"* to get to the final clear-cut answer. It's better to be sure and wrong than not to know. Americans tend not to wait for someone to make decisions that might entail many factors to consider. We think taking action and making mistakes helps us learn, so waiting until you are absolutely certain is considered a waste of time.

This is unlike Asian cultures and more collective cultures, where a consultation with a group is necessary in order to reach a decision. Getting other people's opinions, discussing the pros and cons of the decision, reaching a consensus from colleagues and then making a kind of collective decision often takes more time. The ultimate decision itself may be a conditional yes or no, and not a simple yes and no that many Americans seek.

The Social Grease

Expressions such as "I'm sorry," "please," and "thank you" are often used without giving much thought in order to maintain smooth relationships in the U.S. One Brazilian visitor related her experience of walking down a crowded street. As a man was about to walk past her, he quickly moved to the side of the sidewalk. Without even bumping into her, he said, "I'm sorry" to her a couple of times. The Brazilian found this experience quite common and she thought it was rather odd. Her story shows that the interpersonal space of Americans is perceived to be quite large. The man probably felt that he entered her personal space when he was about to pass her so he apologized to her. Brazilians don't move to the side of the street if they come close to each other when passing and they wouldn't expect an apology either.

Similar to the habit of apologizing in our culture, we say "please" and "thank you" a lot here. We even call them "the magic words." We have a cartoon character, a purple dinosaur called Barney, who teaches young children how to sing a "Please and Thank You" song on his television show. If American children do not say these words automatically when they ask for something or when they have been given something, parents usually remind their children by asking, "What's the magic word?" (please) or "What are we forgetting?" (thank you). These automatic phrases make people feel valued in a society where we like to believe that everyone is equal in status.

Notes

"Americans seem sometimes to believe that if you are a thinker you must be a frowning bore, because thinking is so damn serious."

– Jacques Maritain, French philosopher (1882-1973)

Pride & Prejudice

Here are a few ethnic museums located in the U.S. These museums show both our painful past mistakes as well as our country's ethnic, religious and cultural diversity.

1. Arab-American Museum, Dearborn, Michigan

This museum shows the diversity of the Arab community in the United States. *www.arabamericanmuseum.org*

2. Illinois Holocaust Museum, Skokie, Illinois

This museum displays the Holocaust and modern atrocities in Darfur, Rwanda and Cambodia. *www.ilholocaustmuseum.org*

3. U.S. National Slavery Museum, Fredericksburg, Virginia

A museum that focuses on the role of slavery in the history of the United States. *www.usnationalslaverymuseum.org*

Hate Crimes in the United States

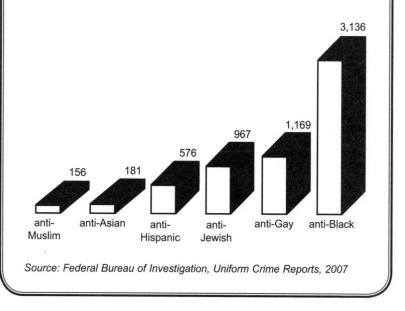

Source: Federal Bureau of Investigation, Uniform Crime Reports, 2007

Chapter 3:

Under Our Skin

I s there such a thing as a pure or true American? Do you mean the Native Americans who were living here before the Europeans discovered them? Today, Indians or Native Americans number less than 1% of the population. Over the course of four hundred years of European contact, those who survived have married people outside their tribe and race. An Indian from a tribe with a low intermarriage rate would be the closest thing to a pure or true American as you could get today.

Christopher Columbus was lost when he landed in America in 1492. He thought he was in India. That's why he called the natives here "Indians." Most of us celebrate the founding of America in a civic holiday called Columbus Day, but for the Indians, it is a Day of Mourning. It marks the beginning of European contact, which brought diseases that killed 90% of their people.

The Native American struggle continues today, long after the Indian Wars officially ended in 1890. Half of the

Home Away from Home

Vietnamese: "Little Saigon" Chicago, Illinois

Arabs: Dearborn, Michigan

Swiss: New Glarus, Wisconsin

Mexicans: Olivera Street, Los Angeles

Greeks: Greektown, Detroit, Michigan

Portuguese: New Bedford, Massachusetts

Koreans: Koreatown, Los Angeles

Cubans: Little Havana, Miami, Florida

Chinese: Chinatown, San Francisco & NY City

Italians: Little Italy, Baltimore, Maryland

Japanese: Japantown, San Francisco, California

Germans: Cincinnati, Ohio

The foreign born make up 12% of the U.S. population. Ethnic neighborhoods are found all across the country as a result of many immigrant groups moving to the U.S. These immigrant communities offer ethnic markets and restaurants. Many of these enclaves also have newspapers and social networking groups.

Native Americans are assimilated into urban areas, the U.S. Census reports, while nearly half of Native Americans still live on reservations.

Some tribes are still fighting to get their land back. Many tribes are suing the U.S. government over land promised to them more than a hundred years ago. Some Indian reservations have set up casinos in the past decade, and are doing financially better than other Indians living on reservations that have no gambling. Reservation Indians are some of the poorest Americans in the country. They have little income and depend on federal government food and money to survive.

Native Americans are also fighting the practice of using tribal names and images for college and professional sports teams. These images reinforce the Indian as a warrior when in reality, most members of the hundreds of Indian tribes were artisans, weavers, pottery makers, and fishermen, among other non-warrior occupations.

It is interesting to note that in the United States the first white colonists tried to capture the Indians and make them into a cheap labor force, but research shows that most Indians got sick and died from the diseases that Europeans brought. Other Indians escaped and hid in the forests and vast land they knew better than the Europeans. If the colonists had been successful in capturing and enslaving them, the United States might have a very different population today. It might have looked similar to the Latin America of today, with a large majority of mestizos and indigenous languages actively spoken.

But it didn't happen that way. Largely unsuccessful with the Indians, the European colonists looked to importing slaves from West Africa as a source of cheap labor in order to sell their sugar and tobacco to international markets.

As soon as the slave trade began in this country, interracial marriage was banned. Puritan colonists from the Protestant Church wanted to keep their people pure of other races. In Brazil and Spanish America, however, the

Roman Catholic Church was the dominant institution and allowed more mixing of the races. So today, race isn't as much of an issue in Brazil and Latin American countries as it is in the United States.

African Americans are the only immigrants that were forced to come here, arriving chained to a ship. They were inspected and bought like property. The master stripped them of their West African names, gave them any first name they wanted, and didn't even bother to give them a last name.

Many African Americans were not permitted to have families. Husbands, wives, and children were sold to different slave masters. Some slave masters would rape African women, and after the African slave gave birth to the child, they could be kept with the master's family or be bought and sold. It is from this history that African Americans face an enormous task if they want to trace their history; some learn that it often stops at a slave ship.

How do we identify ourselves in such a mixed culture? The paradox consists of having a mental map with landmarks of Indian removal and black slavery, yet history books are filled with success stories of immigration and assimilation. While European Americans may tell you a story of assimilation, for Native and African Americans, there are other stories to be told of removal and separation.

Many foreigners believe in the myth that the United States is a melting pot or a mix of races blended together to make one nation, a myth which ignores our long history of trying to keep races apart.

What melting pot? If our nation poses for a class picture, other people might see faces of every color, but to the American eye, it would be developed in black and white.

We still have segregation. Though segregation is illegal, we still have inner-city schools made up largely of blacks, Hispanics, and other minorities, while suburban schools are mainly white. We have neighborhoods where an African

American family moves in and the whites move out.

The American government has always divided its people by race. When the U.S. Census began counting people in 1790, it divided people into free white men and women and slaves.

Today, the United States divides its 300 million people into five major categories of White, African American, Hispanic, Asian, and Native American. In the 2000 Census, the government let us choose more than one category of race. This national census had 63 racial categories to check your mixed blood compared to the traditional five. For the first time in history, the U.S. government recognized mixed blood in this country.

Racial categories, however, make no sense even with more choices. White and black are based on skin color. We are not white and black. These are arbitrary identifiers. Whites are all various shades of skin colors, yellowish brown, pinkish white, copper brown, olive-skinned, and many of us are closer to brown although we don't call ourselves Brown.

The commonly-used term of African American is based on a continent where blacks were forced to leave. Hispanic is a collective term based on language, or whether the person speaks Spanish. The Asian category refers to all Taiwanese, Chinese, Japanese, Koreans, Indians from India, and any other nationality that comes from the continent of Asia.

The U.S. government identifies us one way, but we have chosen to identify ourselves in our own ways.

Although the federal government puts everyone together into an umbrella term, Hispanic, Mexican Americans don't think of themselves as Hispanic. They are Latinos or Chicanos. They often ask each other what city their relatives were originally from in Mexico. Are you a Poblano, Oaxacan, or Chilango from Mexico City? These regional origins are reflected in the music and the food of the Mexican communities living in metropolitan areas throughout the United States.

The true number of Hispanics is hard to measure. The term Hispanic is considered an ethnic group by the federal government, and not a race. Hispanics can be of any race, black or white.

Other nationalities falling into the Hispanic category identify themselves from their respective nation of origin. So you have Puerto Ricans, Cubans, and Salvadorans, all retaining their native country's identity and food customs.

Asian Americans call themselves Asians and ask each other which generation they are from, giving each other a reference point as to how long they have been in the United States. It is a marker for assimilation as well. Are you first generation, second generation or third generation? The language of Taiwanese, Cantonese, and Japanese is usually understood by the first generation but not always spoken very well. By the second generation, it is understood and spoken less, and by the third generation it is often lost entirely.

Asians also identify with other Asians by the values they share, with education being one of the most important values. It is common for Asian parents to pay for their children's college education including graduate school. This financial support throughout their childhood and college sets this minority group apart from other groups, including whites. This investment in their children is seen as a circle. Parents will take care of their children and in turn, adult children will someday take care of their elderly parents. This respect for the parents often strongly connects the Asian community.

African Americans feel a natural affinity to other blacks through their history of not being treated equally. How blacks speak often identifies how well they have adapted to the mainstream white majority. Blacks have an insider language with their black brothers and sisters. They are often bilingual, able to use standard English in schools but talk the slang with their black friends and family at home.

Unfortunately, many foreigners are afraid of blacks when they come to the United States because they have never personally known a black person. Or they are prejudiced against them because television images of gangs and street life reinforce negative stereotypes.

Native Americans identify themselves by tribe as Cherokees, Sioux, Chippewas, Iroquois, Apaches, and Navahos. There are more than 700 tribes in the United States, though the federal government only recognizes about 542 of them. Each tribe has a certain blood requirement; for example, 1/4 Indian can usually qualify you for a certain tribe.

The number of Indians has actually increased over the last decade as some tribes fight over how they will distribute the gambling revenue from the numerous casinos set up on Indian reservations. For example, the Cherokees don't need any proof of their ancestry as it is strictly based on self-identification. This tribe now registers as the largest Indian tribe in the United States.

When you ask European Americans where they are from, they speak in percentages too. They are 1/4 German, 1/4 Irish and the other half English. If you probe deeper and ask them what city in Europe, they usually do not know. Great, great grandmother left behind all her relatives in the old country. Family surnames were often shortened or misspelled by the Immigration Officer when relatives stepped off the boat. Their mother tongue suddenly became a private language of the past, to be only spoken at home, and given up in one or two generations. It is this history, this mental map, that European Americans have of their ancestry. No elaborate family trees, only a sketchy story retold to those who ask. A family history that is usually passed down orally from one generation to the next by an older relative.

Whites don't use the term European American because they make up the majority of people in the United States. They feel no need to be identified by the continent of origin. Since European Americans are the only group in the United States to have a history of assimilation rather than discrimination, their history is the one written down in our history books and taught in our schools.

All this ethnic diversity in the United States surprises foreigners, especially the Koreans and Japanese. These nuances and distinctions of racial identity in the United States do not exist in highly homogenous cultures. Ancestors have an important role in Confucianism and many Koreans and Japanese have a huge family book that traces their ancestry back many generations. They have elaborate ceremonies remembering their ancestors on the day they died, with special food and religious rites. Names have special significance and help trace your ancestry, too.

Some Americans have regular family reunions that are centered around a holiday or an annual picnic. A family tree may even be created by a relative that has researched the family history. Still, talking about our ancestors is not very common in the United States. Our future plans are much more popular topics for conversation. Now you know why Americans prefer to look to the future because we know little about our past.

New Immigration Trends

Though many people think of immigrants resettling in cities on the East and West Coast of the U.S., the newly-arrived are largely passing up the coastal cities and settling in Midwestern and the Southern cities today. This influx of immigrants to new regions of the U.S. has caused a kind of social revolution in terms of our traditional immigration patterns. St. Paul Minnesota, in particular, has the highest number of Hmong refugees. Omaha Nebraska has the largest Sudanese population. The Southeast is also experiencing a revolutionary social restructuring in six states. The states of North Carolina, Arkansas, Georgia, Tennessee, South Carolina and Alabama all have dramatically increased their Spanish-speaking immigrants in the last decade!

Notes

"I look to a day when people will not be judged by the color of their skin, but by the content of their character."

– Martin Luther King, Jr., civil rights leader (1929-1968)

American Families

The typical American family is no longer the husband, wife and two children. Families come in all shapes and sizes in the U.S.

People who live alone may have been married, widowed, divorced or may eventually marry. Single parents may be single by choice or may have been counted as married before.

Gay couples can be counted as individuals living alone or unmarried couples living together.

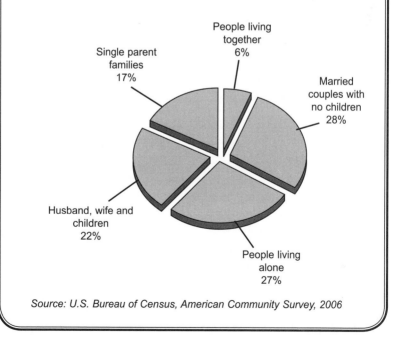

Single parent families
17%

People living together
6%

Married couples with no children
28%

Husband, wife and children
22%

People living alone
27%

Source: U.S. Bureau of Census, American Community Survey, 2006

Chapter 4:

Family Ties & Knots

W hat is the American family? It's the single mother with children, the grandmother who is raising the grandchild, the couple who chooses not to have children, the unmarried couple living together, and the lesbian or gay couple who adopt a child. Many American families do not fit the stereotype of a traditional family with the husband, wife, and children. Even when we have married couples with children, we might have husbands who stay home while their wives support the family.

No wonder most of us feel uncomfortable when asked about our families when we first meet people. These questions are considered very personal because we have mixed feelings. How will we be judged by those who have traditional views of a family? We feel defensive about the family question. It's not easy to explain the complicated patterns of American families when we do not know the expectations of the other person.

Some state governments are slowly recognizing some

of these new arrangements of families. Currently, there are a handful of states that favor same-sex couples. The states of California, Hawaii and New Jersey have domestic partnership laws that give same-sex couples the rights of traditional marriages. These laws follow the trend of nations such as Germany, France, Sweden, Denmark, and Canada, which recognize new forms of partnerships. Some private employers use the new terms *significant other, partner* or *companion* in redefining their policies regarding health insurance. Gay couples can legally marry in six states in the U.S.: Massachusetts, New Hampshire, Connecticut, Maine and Iowa. The number of states allowing gay marriage will likely grow in the future.

By the time American women marry and decide to have children, many have been on birth control for many years. If they have waited until their late 30's or 40's, some women may face problems having children. They undergo expensive fertility injections, and some couples are successful in having children with this treatment.

Other couples give up trying to have children naturally and decide to adopt. In American adoptions, the birth parents choose the adoptive parents based on pictures, biographical information, and meetings. American birth parents also have a period of time in case they want to change their minds about giving up their child for adoption. However, in international adoptions, adoptive parents have little or no involvement with birth parents. The waiting time to adopt a child from overseas tends to be shorter than for a domestic adoption.

Guatemala is the top source of adoption in the United States. Many children also come from China, Russia and Ethiopia. However, international adoptions have sharply dropped in the U.S. since 2007 when many countries signed the Hague Adoption Convention, a multilateral agreement which aims to monitor adoption practices throughout the world.

Adoptions from South Korea have also decreased in recent years because the South Korean government is promoting and supporting domestic adoption. There are also tougher requirements for adoptions in China, which has been the leading source of international adoptions for American families.

Single women are adopting children in growing numbers too, as it is becoming more socially acceptable to be a single mother. The current Census figures show that adopted children make up about 2.5% of America's 65 million children. Many of those children are adopted by their relatives or their stepmother or father.

Three million children are being raised by gay and lesbian parents in the United States, estimates a gay rights organization, The Family Equality Council. The culture is deeply divided on gay marriages and gay parenting. The future will show how willing Americans are to accept children with two moms or two dads.

Another kind of family that is on the increase is the American childless couple, where the woman is physically able to have children but chooses not to. Many childless couples want to maintain their flexible lifestyles. Some may want to travel or dedicate themselves entirely to their careers and don't want the commitment involved with raising children.

Tying the Knot

How easy is it to be married if you are heterosexual? Very easy. In Las Vegas, Nevada, 24-hour chapels will marry you without a waiting period. Weddings are the second largest industry in Nevada after gambling. You can get married in a helicopter, a hot air balloon, or by a clerk dressed up as Elvis Presley.

When you come back for the ceremony, you need at least one witness to be present. Some City Halls even provide the witness. The marriage ceremony lasts about ten minutes. The total cost to get married in this civil way is $50-$100 for the marriage license and ceremony.

Once married, the inequality of the sexes in the United States emerges. Despite the idea of equality in our heads, in practice, most American men and women are not even close to being equal when it comes to caring for their children and doing housework. Polls have shown that American women today still do most of the housework and cooking just like generations ago. The mother typically disciplines during the day while threatening to tell the father later. If the mother tells the father what happened during the day, the child might get another scolding from the father when he gets home.

Untying the Knot

It is well known than almost half of our marriages end up in divorce. It is a bit ironic that when we get married, we worry about getting divorced, and that when we buy a new home, we often worry about the price we will sell it for in the future.

You may be surprised to learn that the U.S. divorce rate has actually fallen in the past decade to around 43%. Though it still remains high, we do not have the highest divorce rate in the world. The United Nations reports that Russia, Sweden, Finland and Britain have higher divorce rates than the United States

Why does nearly one in every two marriages fail in the United States? The American divorce rate might be a reflection on how relatively easy it is to get a divorce in the United States. In most states, if the couple has no children, they must be separated six months to a year. However, if children are involved, it could be many years if one partner is unwilling to divorce. State laws vary on the grounds for divorce but most states have "irreconcilable differences." You don't have to explain the circumstances that led you to file for the divorce. You just say you have differences that can't be resolved.

The high divorce rate may also reflect how socially acceptable it is to get a divorce in this country. The social stigma of being divorced is practically gone in the United States, as it was witnessed recently in Southern California. A Volkswagen was decorated with streamers and bright yellow flowers. Painted in big black letters and stuck on the back of the car was a sign "Just Divorced." The woman was honking her horn and waving to people in absolute joy. As people drove past her, they were waving back.

In the United States, after couples divorce, some couples remain friends if they have children. The child spends the week with the Mom and a couple of weekends a month with Dad. The child's bag is usually packed and ready to go to Mom or Dad's house as he or she shuttles back and forth to the parents' homes.

Other single mothers raise their children themselves as many dads disappear after getting divorced. It may be that the mother wants the husband as far away as possible. More often than not, though, it is because the dads do not want to pay the money to support their children or former wife. Dads who disappear in order to escape paying child support or alimony are called *dead-beat dads*.

Not paying child support is such a serious problem for families in this country that many states have recently passed new laws connecting the driver's license data network to court-ordered payments. So if a *dead-beat dad* applies for a driver's license in another state or even renews his license in the same state, the government now has a record of where he lives. If he has been ordered to pay child support, the state will begin to collect child support payments by deducting money from his paycheck.

The U.S. divorce system differs greatly from other countries' practices. In many Muslim countries, divorce is as easy as the man saying he wants a divorce in front of a witness and the couple is divorced. In Japan, being divorced is especially difficult for women, many of whom must find a job for the first time in their lives. Finding an apartment for the divorced partner in such an expensive city such as Tokyo is also another challenge. In Korea, it is common for the husband to get custody of the children of the divorced couple. The husband's parents usually raise the children rather than the mother, as is the custom in the United States.

In other countries with lower divorce rates, living apart without filing divorce papers is more common than here because of the financial or legal burden placed on the divorcing couple. There may be pressure from the family, the religion, or the society not to officially divorce. For whatever reason, couples stay permanently separated without actually filing papers for divorce. In these countries, the permanent separations are not counted as divorce, and in turn, the nation's official divorce rate might be lower than those countries that readily get divorced with papers.

Many people blame our high divorce rate on the fact that 60% of American women work, and therefore fail to balance motherhood with their careers. However difficult it is to maintain this balance, this only partly explains the high divorce rate in the United States

People from other countries often think American women dominate their men in a relationship, but this is more of a media stereotype seen in TV programs than a reflection of the reality. Many married women are independent from their partners rather than dominating them. You see television sitcoms with the woman slapping her husband on the cheek when she is upset by something he said. In the television series *Spin City*, you saw Heather Locklear slapping Michael Fox. In movies, Andie McDowell slapped Bill Murray in *Groundhog Day*, and Gwyneth Paltrow slapped Colin Firth in *Shakespeare in Love*. For entertainment, a woman slapping a man may produce laughs for a sitcom or dramatic tension for a movie. On the screen, the man does not do anything to the woman. But if this happens in real life, a man usually hits back and the woman most often gets hurt.

Historically, American women have been independent from the time the first colonists came to the United States Women often came with their husbands and left their extended family behind in Europe. In rural America, they had no choice but to work alongside their husbands to clear the land, plant food and build houses for themselves and neighbors.

There was a quantum leap in women's independence in the 1940's when American men went to Europe and the Pacific to fight in World War II and women took over men's jobs in factories. When the war was over in 1945 and men returned to reclaim their positions, some women stayed in the working world. Even the women who returned home to be housewives had experienced the world of work for the first time, and many liked it.

The need to work in an undeveloped land and later in factories was followed by the women's rights movement of the 1960's and 1970's. Women no longer felt the social pressure to stay married if it was a bad marriage and filed for divorce in record numbers. Between 1962-1981, the number of divorces tripled in the United States. Birth control and the sexual revolution delivered the final blow to the traditional family. The husband, wife, and two children mold broke into many little pieces, and today families are regrouped into the many unconventional arrangements.

The Western tradition of choosing your own marriage partner based on the falling in love, or what Asians often call "love marriages," is not practiced everywhere in the world. Some families still choose to have arranged marriages in India, Japan, and some Middle Eastern countries. Many Indian families who are living outside of India often wish to marry other Indians. Contrary to popular belief, arranged marriages are usually not forced marriages between strangers today. These marriages are often planned with the consent of the couple, and are a way for parents to actively get involved in choosing a mate for their son or daughter. Families who support arranged marriages claim these kinds of marriages last longer because the backgrounds of the partners are investigated and known beforehand.

Notes

"The thing that impresses me the most about America is the way parents obey their children."

– King Edward VIII, English King (1894-1972)

If you open an American fridge, you'll find...

How We Cook:

We tend to season our food by making it spicier or tastier by adding condiments to the food *after* cooking.

This way, Americans can change the flavor of the food according to their personal taste.

Unlike many other countries, the cook uses seasonings and spices *while* cooking.

- *ketchup – we put it on just about everything.*
- *honey mustard*
- *mayonnaise*
- *soy sauce*
- *salad dressings – two to three bottles.*
- *salsa or hot sauce*
- *steak sauce*

Chapter 5:

Eat Now, Pay Later

W hy are so many Americans overweight? This is the land of light beers, diet Cokes and watery coffee. With so many sugar-free and non-fat foods on our store shelves, we should all be as thin as a pencil.

The paradox is that Americans have a love/hate relationship with food. On one hand, we will eat anything and everything. On the other hand, we feel guilty about most of what we eat. We think about dieting all the time, "I'm on a diet," or "I'm watching my weight," is a permanent fixture in the American mind. It also makes up a good part of our daily conversation. "I know I shouldn't but . . . I don't have much willpower today." For women especially, their self-esteem often depends on how much they weigh.

Sixty percent of American adults are overweight. How Americans became so overweight is complex. It deals with many trends and habits we do not even think about: eating alone, eating fast, and eating while doing another activity.

Eating a meal with someone else is disappearing in the United States. When we eat alone, we eat to fill up our bellies instead of stopping to converse and savor the taste. Many people eat an entire meal in five minutes. We are losing not only our conversational skills, but also our table manners when we eat alone. We lick our fingers, chew with our mouths open, and mix food on our plate in a way we would not normally do in public.

We eat while doing other activities instead of concentrating on the meal. We grab a bowl of cold cereal while reading a newspaper. Some of us don't even take a lunch break. We do errands or eat lunch at our desk. Or we buy take-out from a restaurant and eat our sandwiches while walking back to the office. Others do not get out of their cars at all, but instead, use a drive-thru window of a fast-food restaurant. They order a hamburger and fries and eat their meal while driving.

On the way home from work, many of us buy dinners from the deli section of the grocery store. When we get home, some of us turn on the TV. We may eat dinner watching TV. If we work on the computer in the evening, we may snack while on the computer. Since our minds are not on the food when we eat a meal, we may overeat.

We focus on the quantity of food rather than the quality of the food in the United States. This is reflected in the adage, "the more, the better." At movie theaters, concession stands sell you enormous tubs of popcorn, giant sodas, and monster boxes of candy. Advertisers know how Americans value size. That's why they print the appropriate buzz words on packages to sell their snack foods "Super size," or "Now 50% more." "Two for one specials," "Buy one and get one free," are examples of how we buy food for its quantity.

You can see how Americans value quantity when we order in a restaurant. We frequently ask the waitress about the size of the dish. "How big is it?" We rarely ask whether it's fried, boiled, steamed, whether the dish contains cream or butter, or the kind of seasonings used to make the dish. These are more quality-type questions, but we are more interested in the quantity of the food. If we did ask questions regarding the quality of the food, the waitress might think we are customers that are hard to please. It wouldn't be surprising if the waitress knows little about the basic methods of preparation or ingredients of a dish, either.

When you order an appetizer or a side dish because you want a small portion, the server will look at you strangely or your friends will even pressure you to have a full meal. Many people who want less food make up a medical excuse. "I can't eat this or that because I'm on medication," or "I just ate a huge breakfast or lunch."

So you order in a restaurant and your plate comes to your table. The food is piled up as high as Mount Fuji. Restaurants often serve enough food for three people in one order. This makes us feel good. First, we feel good that we are unable to eat it all. We can ask for a doggie bag to take the rest home. Some of us eat the food in the doggie bag as soon as we get home. We feel guilty about eating it all in front of everyone in the restaurant, or maybe we were full before, but twenty minutes have gone by and our needs have changed. A smaller number of us save it for tomorrow's lunch or dinner. This also makes us feel good as we feel there is value in eating out. We have just spent our money in a restaurant not for one meal but for a meal and a half.

Americans are also overweight because they snack between meals. Snacks are everywhere. Overweight people fail to stop munching on snacks when they want to lose weight. They simply buy snack food that is fat-free, salt-free or sweetened with a no calorie sweetener instead of sugar.

There is a non-fat potato chip bag that lets people eat the whole bag for 0 grams of fat. So Americans have the notion they are eating less. Only 200 calories for the whole bag of potato chips! They eat the whole bag. You see this logic in fast food places too. People order a hamburger, a large fries and a giant *diet* Coke.

Americans buy junk food because it's cheaper. Why is it that a bag of apples cost more than one huge bag of doughnuts? Or a liter of Coke is less expensive than a small bottle of water? If something is too expensive, Americans won't buy it.

In lower-income neighborhoods and inner cities, you only find expensive convenience stores like a *7-11*. We seldom see grocery stores with fresh fruit and vegetables. Coupons in the local newspaper are mainly for packaged, canned, frozen or junk foods. There are never coupons for discounts on fresh fruit and vegetables.

Food has been taken out of the area of nourishment for the body and into the universe of entertainment. Food is fun. Advertisers shape and package food into something that looks like a toy. There are purple and green crackers shaped like goldfish. We have green ketchup and blue Pepsi. We have peanut butter and jelly swirls in a jar. Breakfast cereals are coated with peanut butter and chocolate and taste more like candy than cereal. Cereal boxes hide toys at the bottom. McDonald's and Burger King give away dolls and action figures so children will beg their parents to go to their fast food outlets for the toy.

Many of us eat a sandwich for lunch "on the run," or while walking and doing errands. Actually, eating while doing something else goes back to the very origin of the name sandwich. Back in 1762, an English nobleman was too busy gambling to stop to eat. Duke Earl of Sandwich didn't want to get his fingers greasy while gambling so he ordered a piece of beef between two pieces of bread. Soon others began to order "the same as Sandwich!" The U.S. has made its own regional varieties.

How do I love the sandwich?

We borrowed the *baguette* or long narrow bread from the French and the *ciabatta* or the oblong bread from the Italians and have made them into our own American sandwiches with names such as hero, grinder, hoagie, subway, submarine, and torpedo. Of course, we have our packaged loaves of airy slices from the supermarket too. But here are some regional varieties of sandwiches.

Let me count the regional ways...

Sioux City, Iowa – Loose Meat Sandwiches, Taverns, & Sloppy Joes: A ground beef mixture served hot on a hamburger bun. With the spicy tomato sauce added, they are called Sloppy Joes because these sandwiches are messy or "sloppy" to eat.

New Orleans, Louisiana – Po-Boy (shortened version of "Poor Boy"): A submarine sandwich – slices of roast beef or ham stuffed in a French roll. It used to be an inexpensive meal.

New York City & Omaha, Nebraska – Reuben: Corned beef on rye bread with Swiss cheese, sauerkraut, and Thousand Island Dressing. This sandwich is buttered, grilled, and served warm.

Boston, Massachusetts – Fried Clam Roll (popular all over New England): Clams dipped in batter and deep fried, and put in a hot dog bun with tartar sauce and a slice of lemon.

Philadelphia, Pennsylvania – Philly Cheese Steak Sandwich: Top round steak grilled and covered with melted American or provolone cheese, served on a hero roll with grilled onions on top.

Convenience Foods

Food in this country is very convenient. Entire meals are frozen for you. International visitors visit a supermarket and are shocked at the aisles of frozen food. The need to transport food from one part of the country to another arose in the 1930's and the idea of frozen food was born. Then the microwave oven came into existence in the 1970's. This invention shrank the preparation time of heating up a frozen food tray in the conventional oven and took convenience to new heights. It no longer takes forty minutes in a regular oven. Now we can have our food ready in a microwave minute.

Who actually eats these frozen foods? Many people buy frozen food because they are pressed for time. Such people range from college students who lack kitchen facilities to people who are on diets. Those trying to lose weight often buy a Weight Watchers food tray or a Healthy Choice Gourmet. They pop these instant meals into the microwave for lunch and know exactly how many calories they are consuming for their calorie-restricted diet. In this way, dieters don't have to worry about portion control. Frozen meals like the Stouffers food trays provide dinner for many of our elderly who live alone. Senior citizens eat these meals because they want to be as independent as possible yet do not want to cook.

Tempting food smells are everywhere in the United States. The smell of grease from the frying of hamburgers and french fries can be sniffed as you pass the local McDonald's or Burger King. Food smells are entering cosmetics and toys. Shampoos and body creams are fruit-scented and kid's magic markers smell like lemons, strawberries and grapes.

American Food

What is American food? Is it only hamburgers and hot dogs?

Americans copy food from every country you can think of. Immigrants come here with native recipes and good intentions of making the identical dish here. It's like putting an authentic, detailed recipe in the photocopy machine. *Voila!* A simplified version of the dish comes out the other end.

Unfortunately, the dish is missing key ingredients because they aren't available in the United States. Americans usually want to shorten the cooking and preparation methods. The result comes out tasting quite different from the native dish and foreigners easily recognize the difference in taste. This is not Chinese or Italian food. It's the American version of it. You can find these copycats of international cuisine in restaurants throughout the United States. Even in small towns, there is at least one Chinese or Italian restaurant somewhere. But take note, you will usually eat the altered photocopy version, not the original.

A teacher's visit to Scripps Aquarium with international students revealed strong cultural differences regarding food. The Japanese students peered into the tanks and politely pointed out how delicious the octopus, squid and other fish species were. To them, the beauty and mystery of coral reefs and fauna were nice, but concentrating on the fish as an edible source of food was better.

Despite the internationalization of food, the rich cuisine of a particular region of the country is still very much alive in the United States. You can find clam chowder in Boston, Cajun stew in Louisiana, Soul food, or grits and greens in the South, and Tex-Mex food in the Southwest. Many Americans also grow up eating the food of their grandparents. If your family has Polish and Italian ancestry, for example, then you probably grew up eating sausage and spaghetti. Food customs are the most enduring foreign customs preserved in the United States.

Of course, there are also the meat and potatoes and the overcooked vegetable as a typical meal. American food is usually seasoned with only a little salt and pepper in

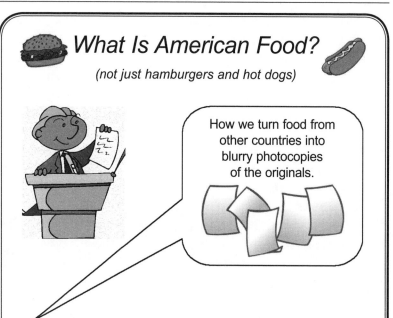

What Is American Food?
(not just hamburgers and hot dogs)

How we turn food from other countries into blurry photocopies of the originals.

Sushi into California Rolls

In the U.S., we took Japanese sushi and made it with less raw fish and stuffed it with more avocado, imitation crab and colorful vegetables. In Japan, the outside of rolled sushi is usually seaweed, but Americans have put the rice on the outside.

Tortillas into Fast Tacos & Burritos

The simple unfried tortilla, which is usually served with a Mexican meal, has undergone a frying fiesta in the U.S. We took the tortillas, fried them, and added an enormous amount of cheese and sour cream.

These lunchtime favorites have changed Mexican plain and basic tortillas into rich, fast-food sandwiches bearing the names of *burritos and enchiladas.*

the preparation. This is why it is considered bland to most foreigners, or even "tasteless."

Although we use very few spices and seasonings *during* the cooking process, we change the flavor *after* with condiments. We pour dressings, ketchup, mustard, soy sauce, Worcestershire sauce, mayonnaise, and hot sauce to improve the flavor of the food. This is the American's way of seasoning food. We make our food as sweet, salty, or spicy as we want. It's not left to the discretion of the cook but a matter of personal choice for the person who eats the food.

It is also typically American that few holidays are tied to a particular food in the United States as they are in other countries. We have no special food for birthdays, funerals or remembering our ancestors as many other countries do. Thanksgiving might be the exception as most people still have turkey, sweet potatoes and cranberry sauce. Many people have eggnog for New Year's Eve and American children go trick or treating for candy on Halloween. We have barbecues for Memorial and Labor Day. However, there are no rituals regarding the preparation of the food, its significance, or the order in which we eat the particular food on these holidays.

Ice Cubes in Our Drinks

International visitors quickly learn the expression, "Water, no ice, please," when they eat out at American restaurants. In fact, Mark Twain was quoted as saying, "The only distinguishing characteristic of the American character I've been able to discover is a fondness for ice water."

Not only do we drink ice water, but iced soft drinks, iced tea and iced coffee. Indeed, to ask for hot water at a restaurant might produce some strange looks by your American waiter.

So why do we automatically put ice cubes in our water and other drinks? Our obsession with iced drinks can be

Italian Pizza into Party Food

In Italy, the most common pizza is a thin 10-inch round tomato and cheese pizza for one person called the *margharita*.

○ Here we have taken this simple tomato and cheese pizza and made it into California cuisine by putting a variety of toppings on our pizza such as broccoli, sausage, anchovies and pineapple.

○ Some Americans even put ketchup on pizza. Pizza is bigger here and comes divided into many slices. Because it's cheap and filling meal, it has become a party favorite.

Chinese Fortune Cookies

These famous cookies were invented in the United States, though there is still some mystery surrounding the origin.

The Chinese '49'ers working on the railroad exchanged these cookies with happy messages inside. They are said to be American copies of Chinese mooncakes.

Sweet Bread into Gooey Doughnuts

Doughnuts are a popular to-go breakfast in the United States. Are doughnuts considered dessert or breakfast foods?

We have taken sweet bread, which is seen in many countries for breakfast, and have put every imaginable filling into them and icing on top of them. Then we have renamed them doughnuts.

traced back to a Boston entrepreneur named Frederic Tudor, who is better known as "The Ice King." He made a fortune by supplying ice to warm weather cities long before artificial refrigeration. Back in the 1800s, Tudor cut ice from frozen ponds in Massachusetts, stored them in insulated ice houses and then shipped the ice to places in the Caribbean, Europe, and India from 1826 to 1892. Through his Tudor Ice Company, Tudor found ways to pack the ice blocks so they would not melt during the ship's voyage.

It was also during this time that Tudor sold ice to wealthy people in the Southern port cities of Charleston, Savannah and New Orleans to help them endure their extremely hot summers. People in the South first started putting ice cubes in their drinks and later, the demand for cold refreshments spread throughout the U.S.

Some Americans believe drinking ice water burns more calories while others think it's bad for the digestive system. Either way, ice water and iced drinks are very popular in the U.S.

A New Zealand resident living in the U.S. told me of how she tried to solve the mystery of the ice-cube maker in her refrigerator. Every time she heard the refrigerator make a noise, she would hurry to throw open the freezer door. She never saw anything. And for the longest time she wondered: how did the ice cubes magically appear in her refrigerator? Finally, she figured it out that her refrigerator came with a built-in ice maker.

English:
The Beauty & the Beast

English is easier to read and write than to speak since it has 26 letters but the actual number of sounds is 35 (11 vowels and 24 consonant sounds).

○ **One English word can have many meanings.**

● You rock! (rock is a slangy adjective to mean great) "She rocks the baby," (rock as a verb); "He threw a rock at her," (rock as a noun); "I listen to rock," (rock as a noun).

○ **New expressions are added quickly** by combining existing language elements or combining a verb with a preposition such as "hang out," "drop off," "hand in" and attaching prefixes to existing verbs: "upload," "offbeat" and "downplay."

○ **English takes from other languages:**

● **French:** action, air, adventure, count, justice

● **West African:** cola, banana, yam, jazz

● **Italian:** piano, umbrella, volcano, artichoke

● **Persian:** paradise, chess, check, and lemon

● **Chinese:** ketchup, silk, tea, chopstick, soy, wok

● **Arabic:** almanac, cotton, orange, sugar, syrup

● **Portuguese:** stereo, monsoon, stead, safari

● **German:** flak, iceberg, cookbook

● **Hindi:** caste, bazaar

● **Japanese:** judo, bonsai, sushi, origami, karaoke

Chapter 6:

English as an Only Language

W hy don't Americans learn a second language? The United States is a leader in international politics and economics yet is one of the most monolingual nations in the world. The answer lies in the roots of American history and geography. We have a history of Americanizing foreigners by making them give up their language and speak English.

The original Americans, the Native Americans, had hundreds of languages, 200 of which still survive today. When the white settlers came west and settled on their lands, Indian tribes moved further west, until eventually there was no more land to move to. The United States government resettled the different tribes into reservations, or they were killed. In the late 19th century, the U.S. government took Indian children away from their parents on the reservations, and put them into boarding schools to force them to assimilate. There, Christian missionaries cut off their long hair, took their tribal clothes, put them in uniform, and forced them to speak English. Indian children were punished if they spoke their own language. Over time, these tribal languages, which were mainly oral languages, have been lost as elders die. Native Americans, in other words, were "Americanized."

Tribal languages, however, left their cultural imprint on the U.S. map. The names of half of the fifty states come from Indian languages. Massachusetts means "at or about the great hill," Illinois is "tribe of superior men," Connecticut signifies "beside the long tidal river." Colonialists needed new words to describe the new animals they met and so took the Indian words *raccoon, caribou, moose, skunk* and *woodchuck,* and English grew.

Just as Indian tribes had many languages, so did black slaves when they came to the United States from Africa. Blacks couldn't speak to each other in their African tongues because slaves were brought from several nations and tribes. In order to survive, slaves learned to communicate through a few slave preachers literate enough to get words from the Bible and house servants who had contact with whites. A kind of abbreviated English with the structure of languages from West African countries developed. This was the root of Black English today.

West African languages such as Mandingo, Kikongo, Temnea, and Wolof have given us many English words such as *banana, jazz, cola, banjo, tote, yam,* and *zombie.*

African Americans often use words with the opposite meaning because in the past, blacks had to encode their language to survive in front of whites. For instance, *bad* is *good* and *kill* means strongly affect someone. These kinds of words were born in America and set American English apart from other countries whose native language is English.

Today, Americans still struggle with the language issue as the number of foreign-born has sharply increased in the last decade. Today, each state determines whether it will have bilingual classes, English as a second language classes, or both. Bilingual classes are classes that are conducted in the immigrant's language, while the student takes English as a second language. During the 2-5 years of bilingual education classes, students are gradually immersed into English classes until they have classes only in English. To further complicate the school language problem, critics of bilingual education believe this method of learning just postpones learning English.

As new immigrants arrive, new laws are made to protect English. The United States started its English language laws state by state in the 1870s in response to the large waves of immigrants from Poland and Italy. Theodore Roosevelt said "Every immigrant here should be required to learn English within five years or leave the country." Today, of the one million immigrants that arrive in the United States each year, a half million legally and an estimated half million illegally, most are Spanish-speakers.

Thirty states have passed English as an Official Language laws. This means government records are to be in English and one cannot demand services in other languages. The following six states require English for driver's licenses: Alaska, Maine, New Hampshire, Oklahoma, South Dakota and Wyoming.

In the workplace, we are divided too. Some employers discourage their employees from speaking another language other than English. On the other hand, retail stores welcome the Hispanic dollar. Bilingual sales clerks are hired and valued because they can wait on a Spanish-speaking customer and increase sales.

Owning the Language

Who owns the language? Is it the government which makes laws telling us which language to use? Or is it the people who use English and change it to meet their needs?

While Americans debate whether they should speak another language, foreigners are increasingly learning

English worldwide. People using English as a second language now outnumber native speakers. There are about 350 million native English speakers compared to 500 million second language speakers. Add all the countries that speak English as a foreign language and it comes to nearly one billion English speakers or nearly one in every seven people on the planet speaks English. It is the primary language of science, computers and business. English is being spoken in Asia as a common business language among the Japanese, Koreans, and the Chinese. The same is true in Mexico and Brazil, where European, Japanese and Korean investment is growing.

In some countries, English is used as a status symbol, a way to show that you are a member of the elite or have studied in the United States. English is creeping into other languages. Italians are quite used to feeling "lo stress", looking forward to "il weekend" or trying to look "cool." Or in Paris, the French will use "le parking, and "les jeans. In Japan, English words such as camera, coffee, and party are often used but are usually pronounced with a heavy Japanese accent.

English borrows from other languages too. English is growing so fast because it seldom rejects foreign words for purity reasons. John Adams, one of our country's founders, suggested creating an American Academy of English to keep the language free from a foreign invasion of words back in 1780. No one listened to him at the time. Consequently, the United States has no group of linguistic scholars combing every word to see if it qualifies as proper English, unlike the "language watchdogs" of France and Spain.

New English words are coined relatively quickly from other languages as immigrants come to the United States. Language and culture cannot be isolated. You can see how the cultural interaction between foreigners and Americans influences English to the extent that it borrows from the new language at the expense of an English word. We use *kaput* from German, *déjà vu* from French, *kudos* from Greek, *kimono* from Japanese, *karma* from Sanskrit and *ketchup* from Cantonese. These foreign words are eventually adopted into the English sound system and make their way into an American English dictionary.

The English language loves brevity and new abbreviations are born as language incorporates new phenomenon. For example, CDs are not only *Certificates of Deposits* but also *compact discs.* PCs could be *personal computers* or *politically correct.*

English is growing as we use English in new ways and create more euphemisms so we do not offend anyone. These shades of meaning are often hard to identify by the international visitor. We use *significant other* to describe a boyfriend or girlfriend outside of traditional family patterns.

Sales associate sounds more prestigious than sales clerk. We are not *at war* but *engaged* in a country. We no longer have a *confrontation* with a person but an *incident,* and the list goes on. English is growing at a rate of a thousand words a year, says Richard Lederer in *The Miracle of Language.* All these new words make their way into the Webster's International Dictionary, bulging at 450,000 words.

Because English is growing and so widely practiced, Americans see little need to learn a foreign language. For their customary two-week vacations, most Americans go to another state or city within the United States instead of traveling to a foreign country. This is why Americans fail to understand the value of learning another language. Census data reveals 20% of children 5 to 17 years old speak another language other than English at home and most of these children are from foreign-born parents who have kept their language.

Forty percent of high school students study a foreign language, yet few speak another language after two to four years of study. Spanish is by far the most popular choice. Americans have taken an interest in learning Spanish ever since advertising agencies began marketing to Hispanics in their language on TV, billboards and the radio.

When Americans travel to Texas, Florida, or Southern California where Spanish is widely spoken, they feel excluded. The irony is that Americans mainly want to learn Spanish to speak with more people *within* their country and not to understand people from *other* countries.

Spanish is primarily a spoken language in the United States. Since many Spanish speakers who were born and raised here were not schooled in the reading or writing of the language, the written form of the mother tongue has been nearly lost. It's like an adopted daughter because we seldom see Spanish written except on billboards or government documents.

The Spanish you hear in Spain and the Spanish you hear in the United States are completely different since the language has become Americanized. We mix English with Spanish all the time. We name this hybrid language Spanglish. We have many nationalities speaking the language here so each ethnic group speaks it differently but all mix it with English.

Americans view culture with blinders on. We have forced immigrants to give up their language but then we celebrate Hispanic Month, African American Month, and Native American month. We charge money to see ethnic groups dance and serve their food at local fairs and school functions. Performing a dance and bringing a dish are acceptable ways to celebrate cultural heritage. In short, the message is clear in America. Show us a foreign culture through food and dance, but not language.

Notes

"We don't just borrow words; on occasion, English has pursued other languages down alleyways to beat them unconscious and rifle their pockets for new vocabulary."

– Booker T. Washington,
American black leader and educator
(1856-1915)

How Do We Make Friends?
Let me count the 16 ways...

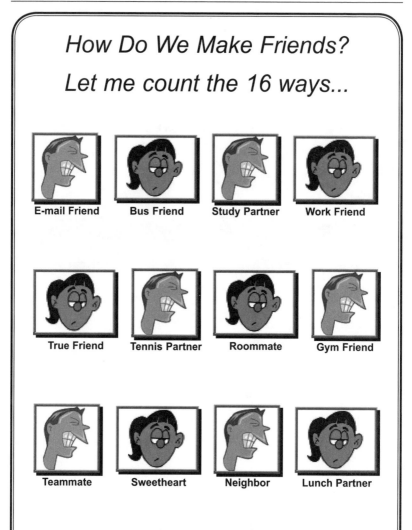

E-mail Friend   Bus Friend   Study Partner   Work Friend

True Friend   Tennis Partner   Roommate   Gym Friend

Teammate   Sweetheart   Neighbor   Lunch Partner

Chess Partner   Family Friend   Classmate   Travelmate

Chapter 7:

True Friends

W hy is it so difficult to make friends with Americans? Many international visitors complain about how superficial Americans are. It's true that after years of knowing people in the United States, you may never be invited to their home. This is unthinkable in other countries.

You have to understand how Americans categorize you, the friend. Many people from other countries misinterpret *being friendly* with *being a friend*.

Being friendly means Americans are easy to approach.

We are open to striking up conversations with a stranger in the grocery line, on the bus or just about anywhere in public. We usually don't ask the stranger's name. The public place simply serves the function of a temporary friendship that dissolves immediately after the chance encounter.

This friendliness also means that if we know you, we might pat you on the back if you are a man, or hug you if you are a woman. Between young people of both sexes, you might be asked to slap the open palm of your hand of another person, "Give me five!" Or you might greet the other person with "a knuckle handshake." The old-fashioned handshake is going out of style for personal encounters among friends, but is still practiced for introductions and business relationships.

Many people from other countries are surprised to see how informal we are. Americans easily put their feet up on a desk or chair or sit down on a table instead of a chair.

Americans love their space, and might overlook other people's needs when they sit or stand. You can see examples of this by how one person may claim two seats on the bus, in the classroom, or the movie theater. One seat is for the person, while the other seat is for their belongings.

When Americans are introduced to each other and the meeting is intentional, we want to know the other person's name right away. Since we don't have titles for most people in the United States, the name becomes the most important factor in identifying a person.

Americans generally dislike personal titles, as we were the nation of rebels that protested against the royalty and the Church of England. In the times of slavery, slaves had to call their white owners "Master." They also were forced to say "Yes Ma'am" and "No Ma'am," and "Yes Sir," and "No Sir," to all whites as a sign of deference to them.

Today, people from the South still retain the "Sir" and "Ma'am" custom, and it has become a polite-sounding tradition to their ears. The American military also retains this form of address as a sign of respect to authority.

We can trace the titles of "Sir" and "Ma'am" to the Middle Ages. Back in the times of 1100-1400, La Dame was a title reserved for women of refinement. La Dame was shortened to Madame, which became later shortened to Ma'am. The male equivalent for a dame was a knight, and was called Sire, which was shortened to Sir. In a formal letter when we don't know a person's name, we still write, "Dear Sir or Madam."

However, to Americans of the North, Midwest, and West, calling them "Sir" and "Ma'am" sounds old-fashioned and too formal. It usually makes them feel uncomfortable because it sounds like one person is putting the other person in a lower position. It goes against the tradition of people considering themselves equal. And if you say "Ma'am" to most women, you will offend them, as many women think this title makes them feel old.

Vestiges of the Middle Ages can also be seen in our notion of "being a gentleman." Chivalry was a code of conduct created by the knights of the Middle Ages to protect the weak, at that time including women, from the warrior class. Today, chivalry is a kind of etiquette that is practiced by men and grants women common courtesies in the United States. For example, it can be pulling out a chair for a woman at dinner, walking on the street side of a sidewalk, opening a door and letting her go into the building first, or giving up a seat on a bus. Feminists dislike this special treatment and say it reinforces the inequality of gender.

What titles do we commonly use in the United States? Some religious, academic, and legal titles are still practiced. Physicians and college PhD's are still called "Doctor." Students of all ages usually address their teachers as Mr. and Miss followed by the last name until they graduate from high school. In court, the judge is still called "Your Honor."

For religious leaders, we still use "Pastor, Father, Rabbi and Imam."

Since many Americans do not have their parents and siblings close by, sometimes they have their children call unrelated close friends with the artificial title of Aunt and Uncle before their first name. This practice is common when close friends serve as a kind of surrogate family.

Yet we don't have titles to express the nuances of relationship with other people, as some cultures do. What about strangers? What do you call the person who forgot her bag on the bus and is now 100 feet (30 meters) away?

Culture: USA

1. **Go to a local high school football or basketball game** and root with the acrobatic cheerleaders.

2. **Take a mini-road trip** to a tourist attraction and stop at a roadside diner.

3. **Order a banana split** at an ice-cream shop.

4. **Watch a live trial** in a local criminal courthouse.

5. **Stop by a local taco shop at night** and ask for a *burrito de carne asada*.

6. **See a house on wheels** by going into a mobile home park and asking to see the inside of a model.

7. **Make a campfire in the countryside** and sing camp songs while roasting marshmallows.

8. **Jog around your neighborhood** in the early morning and see serious dog walkers and runners.

9. **Organize a potluck dinner** at home with no fuss as everyone brings a "pot" or dish to eat.

10. **Have a tailgate party** by packing up your car with picnic food and chairs and having a party in the parking lot before an American game starts.

Or the waitress you have patiently waited for but now feel the need to call her attention? Or what about the person sitting next to you in class who wants to be your friend? What about a special name for your boss, your grandmother or even your mother-in-law?

Unfortunately, we have only one *you* in English. *You* for an individual, *you* for a group, *you* for the president and *you* for the guy next door. We don't have special verb forms or titles to distinguish age, class, stranger, or familiar. That's why your given name becomes all important in American culture. If Americans do not get your name at a party or personal setting, they most likely won't talk to you for any length of time.

If we need to call someone whose name we do not know, and they are far away, we call them by function or identify them by the clothing they wear. We raise our voice and say, "Excuse me, lady in the white dress!" Or, "Excuse me, waitress!" These name and title rules in the United States bring us back to the friendship question. Americans think of friendship in a functional way.

Once Americans know your name and something personal about you, you are usually considered a friend. We have the term "acquaintance" in the English language, but we seldom use it.

Americans make friends easily but it is a rather functional relationship. We put friends in boxes according to where we see them and by the activity shared with them.

If we play tennis, we have a tennis friend. If we know someone at school, we become a school friend. It follows then that we have church friends, family friends, and work friends.

Church friends are rarely invited to play tennis, and tennis friends do not go to church with us. Seldom do we invite one set of friends home to mix with family friends. The friend is in a box with a label on it, "Tennis," "Church," and "Work," and we stow the friend away to be taken out for that one activity.

This functional approach to friendship results in making many friends but knowing few of them well.

Americans move an average of 11 times in a lifetime. The unknown future is always more exciting than today, which may be too familiar. New is equivalent to better in the mind of Americans. We move to get a *better*, not *different*, roommate, job or house. As a result, many Americans keep a distance and choose not to invest the time and the energy needed to build a friendship. Why should I get close to people if they will move away in a couple of years?

Obviously, this presents a particular problem for foreign students and visitors. In the United States for only a short time, meeting Americans usually isn't as much of a problem as getting to know them on a deeper level.

Americans know that the international visitor will leave in the near future, and this will make them very conscious of the amount of time and emotional energy spent on making friends. They might appear warm until the visitor wants to get close to them and then Americans will take a step back. *Not too close.* We might get hurt when the visitor moves away or returns home.

Whatever favors *you do for someone* or whatever favors *you ask of someone* are mentally recorded in an American's mind like a debit or credit card. Simple daily needs that are met by other people have turned into unwritten commercial transactions.

Favors count like money and trading favors is the currency. If you ask an American for a ride in his/her car one day, it is expected that you will do something for that person in the future. If an American invites you to his/her home, you are expected to invite him/her home back at a future date, or at least out to eat. We know we owe someone a favor and must repay him with some kind of favor. We say, "I'm paying you back for the ride you gave me the other day." Or if we haven't done someone a favor yet, we might say, "I owe you."

We are very specific about what we do for others and what people do not do for us. Friendship in this way has become a very commercial idea that most Americans aren't even conscious of. Or, if we are aware of it, we think it is just "being fair." If you do not repay an American you have asked many favors from, the American might feel used, and you might even lose the American friend. On the other hand, if we have asked too many favors of you and realize it, Americans tend to feel guilty and apologize.

With time and persistence, foreigners do make friends with Americans despite the unwritten rules governing friendship. If you do many kinds of activities with an American, including going to each other's house and knowing each other's family, then you are probably considered a "close friend" or maybe a "best friend." You have managed to jump out of the box and transcend the idea of a functional friend. You are able to judge how clean or messy we are, what personal habits we have and what we hang on our walls. Americans think all of this is highly personal and brings friendship to a different level.

Friendship has become a business in the United States in another sense, too, as the word *friendly* is used as a marketing term. It is used to describe who is welcome in a place and who is not. For example, we have restaurants and hotels with signs posted *child-friendly,* which means children are welcome. States are using *business-friendly* to say that their particular state is a good place to do business, with low corporate tax rates, low wages, or few unions. The term *user-friendly* is used for computer interfaces, and even appliances when the machine is easy to use. *Environmental-friendly* is a widely-used term seen on plastic containers that are biodegradable. This term is also used by cosmetic companies such as the Body Shop, a company that does not use animal testing. Can you imagine a Statue of Liberty saying *foreigner-friendly* today?

Chapter 8:

Crazy for Rules

I f this is the land of the free, then why are there so many rules? Do Americans really think they are free with so many laws telling them what they can and cannot do?

Yes, we love to make laws in the United States. We usually make new ones when a private corporation has been sued too many times or some major accident has happened.

Smoking laws were passed when the cigarette maker R.J. Reynolds was slapped with enough lawsuits, safety belts were required after enough accidents, and the age to drink was changed when the number of young people killed in drunk driving accidents rose.

The United States has the most lawyers in the world. We also have one of the highest numbers of people in jail on the planet. We have about 2 million prisoners in jail. Many of these prisoners are not serious criminals but non-violent drug offenders. It costs at least $20,000 a year to house each inmate. Everything we do in the United States has a legal consequence. People walk around in fear. If we break the law, we are afraid someone will either sue us or report us to the police.

Lawsuits arise out of the most ordinary events. When passengers were afraid during a rough American Airlines flight from Los Angeles to New York, they sued the airlines for emotional damages and were awarded $2 million dollars. When an Ohio coach for a Little League baseball team had no wins for the team for the entire season, the father of one of the kids sued the coach for poor coaching. In an Arizona high school, the parents of an English student threatened to sue the school when her daughter failed her English class, so just hours before graduation, the girl was allowed to retake a multiple-choice test. The student barely passed, and was permitted to graduate.

As you can see, making mistakes in daily life here can be not only costly but also turned into a lawsuit in the United States. This is why most Americans, driven by fear of jail or a lawsuit, obey the laws in this country.

Morality is encoded in our civil laws. Rules are posted on signs like the Ten Commandments in the Bible. "No Trespassing" means you can't go on this property. Even if there is no fence, the legal result is the same to an American. You are breaking the law. "No Loitering" means you are not allowed to stay around a store's entrance or parking lot unless you are a customer.

Of course, we are all aware of the no smoking laws. If we aren't, Americans quickly point to the sign and ask, "Did you read the sign?" This is American logic. If the sign is posted, you are informed, and so you will naturally follow the rules.

Drinking Laws

We can drive at age 16, vote at 18, and drink at 21. Drinking must be considered the best as it is saved for last. We can kill someone in a car or get killed in a car accident at 16, we can kill and get killed in the military at 18 but at 21, we can legally have that beer! Now that's a paradox.

Why is this? The reality is that young people under 21 years old *do drink and drive*. The law is made to separate the two activities, drinking and driving, in order to prevent fatal car accidents among young people. The law wasn't meant for the government to be the moral police but to reduce the number of fatal accidents.

What alternatives are there to driving at night in the United States if you want to drink alcohol? It looks pretty grim. In most cities, somewhat undependable local buses mostly stop running in the early evenings and have limited schedules on weekends. Friends can help a little by going along with you and not drinking so they can drive you home. Taxis are usually too expensive to be considered a practical alternative by young people when they drink.

Americans' moral sentiments run strong when it comes to underage drinking and driving. Yet many adults serve alcohol to their teens at home. In fact, many cities have laws that make serving alcohol to underage people at home a crime. Parents or any adult can face a $1,000 fine and up to six months in jail for hosting parties where alcohol was served to underage kids.

Prohibiting drinking until 21 has produced a pattern of drinking that is uniquely American. It is not found in other countries, even though they have a lower drinking age limit. Drinking is more exciting when it's illegal. Not only do American young people drink in their cars and in parking lots, but they also drink with the goal of getting drunk. Since students are not allowed to drink three of their four years in college, drinking privately in your own apartment is fairly common. Young people not only drink secretly but some drink five or more alcoholic drinks in one sitting. This is called binge drinking, and it is pretty common on college campuses. American teenagers have never learned to drink in a social setting so when we finally reach 21 and drink, it turns out to be a selfish kind

of pleasure. It is often a means to get drunk rather than a
way to socialize.

The Legal System

Our legal system is a mystery to many foreign visitors
as they watch famous legal movies such as *A Few Good
Men*, *Witness*, or *Dead Man Walking*. Unlike most real trials,
movies and TV programs are full of high drama and well-
spoken lawyers.

Very few criminal cases actually go to trial, with an
estimated 90% being settled by a plea bargain. A plea
bargain is an agreement between the district attorney and
the defense about the charges. The defendant enters a guilty
plea and a sentence is administered, all without a trial.

The small percent of cases that do go to trial are what
you read about in the newspapers. Most trials are open to
the public, so ordinary citizens can walk into any courtroom
and watch the legal process in action. Unlike television
shows depicting a courtroom full of people, most American
courtrooms are empty except for a few close friends or
relatives of the defendant. Of course, in a highly publicized
case of a celebrity, the major media are there. Then the
courtroom is crowded and sometimes the trial is televised.

Who makes up a jury? Local residents of the city
are called for jury duty. It is an obligation of every adult
American citizen to serve on a jury. People's names are
randomly chosen from voting and driver's license lists.

Nearly every adult is called to jury duty at least once in
his or her lifetime. Nearly everyone tries to get out of it, too.

People dislike going because it can mean taking from
two weeks to several months off work to serve on a trial
jury. As a potential juror, you have no idea how long the
trial will last. Even selecting a jury could take days. Few
employers pay for the time served on a jury. The companies
that do provide a jury service benefit usually pay your
salary for a maximum of two weeks. The court gives jurors

a few dollars a day to pay for transportation and/or lunch money.

Naturally, this virtually unpaid civic duty competes with income-earning jobs, and our jobs usually win. Many Americans write elaborate excuses so they will be excused for jury duty. Others try to get out of jury duty by showing up on the first day of jury selection and answering questions in a way that lawyers will not select them to be a member of the jury. Because of the number of people trying to escape jury duty by the lengthy selection process, many states have new rules that say a jury must be selected in one day.

Race may play a role in producing jury verdicts or the decisions of guilty or not guilty. The highly-publicized Rodney King trial of 1992 is an example. An all-white jury acquitted four white police officers. A predominantly black jury acquitted O.J. Simpson, a famous black athlete accused of murdering his wife and his wife's friend. When a white jury tried Simpson in civil court later, he was found guilty.

Owning Guns

Why do Americans own 65 million handguns? Americans cite the Constitution like no other country in the world. The question should be, why is the murder rate so high in the United States? You can't assume the United States has a high murder rate because so many Americans own guns. It ignores the mentality of Americans and their idea of safety.

Is owning a gun the cause for the high murder rate? An international study on guns and crime in 21 countries found that gun ownership was high in Switzerland, Finland and Canada, but their murder rates were much lower than the United States. But the study also found that guns in the home may lead to suicide, and that they are a threat to women, especially female partners. Owning a gun, however, has little relationship to the murder rates for males or street crime.

Nearly half of the murders in the United States are committed by people who are acquainted with their victims, reports the Bureau of Justice in its 2000 *Homicide Trends in the U.S.* report. *Now that's frightening.* It seems that focusing on guns without finding out why Americans are killing people who are their acquaintances, co-workers and family members is a futile exercise.

Blaming the lack of a conventional family structure does not explain it entirely. Sweden has twice as many births outside marriage than the United States and Canada has about the same as the United States and these countries' murder rates are a fraction of the American murder rate.

Something else causes people to murder other people besides the convenience of owning a gun or the fact that we have many unconventional families.

The high murder rate may be connected to the large gap between the rich and the poor compared to other industrialized countries. The poor and the nonwhite are more likely to be targets of a violent crime than the rich and white. Blacks are almost six times as likely to be murder victims as whites, according to the Bureau of Justice in its 2000 *Homicide Trends in the U.S.* report.

It's clear that Americans feel unsafe in their own country, but this fear is abstract. We have no one in particular in mind. Gun owners argue that they own guns for self-defense. Because the police cannot cover all situations, gun owners say, they are supplementing government protection. Gun supporters also say that owning a gun provides low-income people with a means for self-protection. It's cheaper than an expensive alarm system for a house or the cost of maintaining a security dog. So is it the burglars we are worried about? Then why are students carrying guns to school? With 10% of the schools in the United States reporting serious violence, fear of burglars is a questionable argument.

College students now carry guns too. When polled for the reason college students needed a gun, they said "for self-defense." Against whom? Anybody? This notion of carrying a gun because you are afraid of someone is becoming more widespread. Thirty-one states have right-to-carry laws allowing people to carry a concealed gun on their person.

What we say and what we do are often two different things. We say we want safer cities, but what are we doing to solve the high crime rate? As a culture, we concentrate on the technology, so we say let's get rid of the machinery or the guns and not deal with changing our ideas about violence.

Violent movies such as *Diehard* and *Armageddon* gross millions and qualify as blockbusters in the United States. The culture of violence is built into our American mentality.

We have not learned to resolve conflicts through negotiation and complex talks. We do not know how to manage our anger. When we are mad, we like action, not words. When we kill someone with a gun, the problem is solved in a simple way. After all, that's how movies get rid of the bad guys.

We idolize the cowboy; the loner who has been wronged and waits for no one to help him but takes justice into his own hands. The quick and easy solution in a complex world has turned this country into a people who look to take personal revenge to its extreme of killing, with no chance of that person ever coming back to take revenge on you.

The Death Penalty

Why does the United States have the death penalty? The argument that the death penalty prevents murder is a myth. With that reasoning, having the death penalty in 35 of the 50 states would make the United States the safest country on the planet. We know that's not true.

Some Americans support the death penalty because they are afraid that criminals sent to prison for life will eventually get out of jail based on their good behavior. This rarely happens today, as we have life sentences without parole. This means there is no chance of release. In short, there are no second chances. Yet, people's minds take longer to change.

Though 65% of Americans support the death penalty today, ten years ago, the number of people in favor was around 75%. Americans are questioning the death penalty more today as new information surfaces about innocent death row prisoners who have been wrongfully convicted.

David Protess, a professor at Northwestern University, and his journalism class, investigated death penalty cases and helped free eight death row prisoners who were innocent.

New evidence surfaced, people came forward with confessions, or police work was flawed. These cases have been in the news and have changed some Americans' minds about the death penalty. The notion of the ultimate revenge is expressed through the death penalty. We have a popular expression in the United States, "Don't get mad, get even." Getting even is what the death penalty does. The murderer killed someone, now we kill the murderer.

Over two-thirds of the countries in the world or 138 countries have now abolished the death penalty in law or practice. Just five countries, China, Iran, Saudi Arabia, Pakistan and the US carried out 93% of the known executions in the world in 2008, reports Amnesty International. China leads with the most executions followed by Iran, Saudi Arabia, Pakistan and the United States is in fifth place.

We hear horror stories in the news about killings in Muslim countries of the Middle East, yet when we kill Americans on death row, it is not widely publicized unless the crime was famous. At most, the execution is published as a tiny paragraph in the newspaper. In 2005, the Supreme Court ruled that it was unconstitutional to execute juveniles. Twenty-two defendants had been executed for crimes committed as juveniles from 1976-2005.

Notes

"A jury consists of twelve persons chosen to decide who has the better lawyer."

– Robert Frost, American poet

The American Educational System

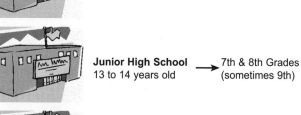

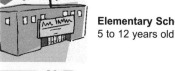

Elementary School
5 to 12 years old   → Kindergarten to 6th Grade

Junior High School
13 to 14 years old   → 7th & 8th Grades
(sometimes 9th)

High School
14 to 18 years old   →

9th – 12th Grades
Freshman 9
Sophomore 10
Junior. 11
Senior 12

College entrance exam (SAT) score
& high school grades must be good.

University / College
Bachelor's degree
4 years, 18 - 22 yrs. old

Community College
Associate's degree
2 - 3 years

Vocational School
Certificate
Weeks to 2 years

University
Master's degree
1 - 2 years

University
Doctor's degree / Postdoctorate
2 - 6 years specialization

Chapter 9:

Shrinking Teachers & Growing Grades

F oreign business executives and scholars who move their whole family to the United States for a year also enroll their children in American schools. Most are surprised to learn their children are ahead of their American classmates in every subject but English, which shows that our elementary and secondary schools must be lagging behind other countries.

How can Americans win Nobel Prizes for mathematics and science while the majority of us have trouble adding restaurant tips and subtracting our balances in our checkbooks? American twelfth-grade students placed well below the international average in both general math and science knowledge when evaluated against international students from 20 other countries in *The Third International Mathematics and Science Study.* Are we spending too much on research to nurture the brightest students and leaving the rest of us behind?

What are American primary and secondary schools

really like? Education in foreign countries is often divided into public and private schools, with a great difference in the quality of instruction. Since 89% percent of American schools are public and only 11% are private, the United States has both good and bad schools in the public and private sector.

The quality of the education usually depends on whether it is a suburban or inner-city school. The affluent, suburban school with plenty of resources, textbooks, and teachers offers a far better education than the large urban school with scarce resources, overcrowding in the classroom, and buildings with roofs that leak. Suburban schools have swimming pools and well-equipped computer labs. Urban schools have security guards and electronic metal detectors.

Of course, if you are a disciplined student, it doesn't make any difference what school you go to, you'll survive on your own academic initiative. But for a large majority of students attending urban schools, they are only waiting for graduation as they suffer through years of mediocre education.

How schools are funded explains how the dual track educational system was created. The city government collects local property taxes from homeowners and gives a percentage of that money to the schools. Schools also receive grants from the state, which carry many conditions, and finally, schools receive a small amount of money from federal government.

In contrast, students' tuition fees, church subsidies and community fundraisers support private schools. When you send your child to a private school, however, you are still financially supporting the public schools through property taxes.

Most students go to the public school closest to their home. Because real estate properties frequently have lower values in neglected urban neighborhoods, inner city schools receive less money from property taxes. This means that there is less money to spend on students, the maintenance of the school building and even textbooks. Some cities have recently offered a "Choice" program where families can send their child to a school outside their neighborhood. However, families usually have to put their child's name on a long waiting list for another school if they live outside of the area. The time a family must wait to be accepted into another school could be a few months or a few years. Some families also use a relative's address in order to send their child to a better neighborhood school.

As a history teacher in a large inner city school in New York City, the great gap between suburban and urban schools was easily noticeable. The high school, located in a working class neighborhood in Queens, had a population of 3,000 racially-mixed students.

Most teachers did not have enough textbooks to give the students, so copies were made from the teachers' textbook and individual chapters handed out to students. Some teachers had enough textbooks but still did not distribute them because students would not bring them to class or would destroy them.

Indeed, the copy room in the school's basement became a very important place for teachers needing copies.

Teachers paid for their own copies most of the time, since a copy order needed to be filled out two days in advance to get copies from the school.

Some students came to school with weapons, but the teachers didn't want to know who they were. If they knew which students had them, it would make them responsible for reporting them and later face possible retaliation from the student.

Every classroom in this New York City school had a telephone. The telephone had a direct number to the security guards who patrolled the hallways. If you kicked a student out of your class because of bad behavior, you would call a security guard or the dean, who are the people in charge of discipline in high schools. The dean would

School Dress Code

No hats or headgear.

No ripped clothing.

No shirts with obscene sayings.

No baggy pants.

No clothing with a sports team logo.

No shirts with religious symbols.

No sunglasses.

No armbands.

No clothing with drug, alcohol, or tobacco references.

To prevent students with oversized shirts and baggy pants from hiding weapons, many schools have instituted a dress code like the above. Because fights have broken out over designer jackets and athletic shoes in schools, school uniforms are also growing popular in schools.

usually come, take the student out of the class and bring them to his office. Then the student would return to class the next day with the same kind of behavior.

In suburban schools, the school environment may be different. There are usually enough resources, including textbooks, well-equipped computer laboratories, and large recreational facilities. However, discipline and dress code problems exist in suburban schools as well, but perhaps not to the degree of the urban schools.

How do we break this vicious circle? The teachers have very little power today. It's next to impossible to kick out a student with a behavior problem in public schools. The number of students who show up each day determines how much money the school receives from the state and federal government. Teachers, therefore, must record attendance in two separate places to have a permanent record for the school. If a student is kicked out, the school loses money.

For these disruptive students, the duty of teachers is to call the parents and report their behavior. Every teacher has five or six classes and by the end of the day, has a long list of students' names. Teachers spend quite a bit of time calling the students' parents. Many times, family members are not home or do not answer the phone. Still, teachers must record the phone call, which leaves them feeling helpless because of their failure to reach anyone.

Some American parents are not available to punish their children. They are working. Many parents are away most of the day and students are raising themselves. With no one home until evening, misbehaving students are seldom held accountable. The teachers are forced to act like their parents and less like teachers. Meanwhile, for students who really want to learn, it is a frustrating experience because one or two problem students are constantly interrupting classes.

Teachers feel helpless when they want to change the system. They become stressed and tired, or what we call "burned out." Some teachers turn apathetic or hyper-critical of students and the whole school system. A good number of teachers leave and start over in other professions, despite all the benefits and vacation time they will be sacrificing.

Even when most schools have a "zero tolerance" policy of automatically kicking out any student caught possessing weapons or drugs, it's still hard to kick a student out. Schools fear parents will demand equal access to education for their child and if the child is not allowed back, parents may threaten to sue them.

Who controls the schools and sets policies? Since American schools are very decentralized, a group of community leaders called The Board of Education makes the rules for the school. This group of local residents decides the textbooks to be used for the area schools, rules of behavior, and resolves serious problems between a teacher and a student.

In many schools, students cannot wear hats or caps of any kind as they might hide drugs in them. Every school makes its own policy toward appropriate school dress. Public schools have been recently adopting uniforms for a dress code, a custom usually reserved for private schools. This change has been an effort to reduce gang clothing.

The principal of the school and the Board of Education have most of the power over the school while parents have little control as to what the student learns and many parents feel powerless if they want to change the rules of the school.

Students form little groups in American high schools. This is one institution where you easily see the segregation of races. In the cafeteria or while students are changing classes, you will see the Mexican Americans in one group, the African Americans in another, the Asians with other Asians, and the whites in their separate group. Some students mix with other students outside their group, but it is not very common.

The schools themselves divide students academically into groups called "tracking" and you follow this academic path throughout your school years. There are Gifted and Talented programs for the very bright kids, Advanced Placement for the college-bound kids, vocational programs for the average kids, and Special Education classes for the slow to learn or students with behavior problems.

Grade inflation is a serious problem in most American schools. Teachers are under tremendous pressure to give high grades whether or not they reflect the student's true academic ability. Many students demand an "A" or a "B" from the teacher these days, and if the grade is anything less, students want to discuss the situation.

For example, if students show up for class, they may get a "C" just for their good attendance. If students do the slightest bit of homework and come to class, they may receive a "B." The full grading scale from "A- F" is seldom used. Teachers rarely fail students for their academic ability because they are under pressure from administrators to pass as many students as they can. If teachers fail students, students may drop out of school and that means less money for the school in the end.

In an effort to combat grade inflation at the college level, Princeton University has instituted a policy in 2004 whereby academic departments will ration the number of As given out to students. Faculty may give A-plus, A or A-minus to no more than 35 percent of the grades given to students, compared to 46 percent of the time in recent years.

Grade inflation can also be seen on the high school level, according to the College Board Report of 2001. The College Board studied American students' SAT scores in 2001 and in 1991. Students with A averages made up 28% of SAT test takers in 1991 compared to 42% in 2001, yet students today have lower SAT test scores than a decade ago. Some high school graduates who have received scholarships because of their grades have even had to take remedial college classes.

Social skills are valued as much as academic abilities in

Social Cliques

High school students often belong to many social groups. Two of the most common groups are listed below.

Jocks are the athletes. They are usually the most popular students and have status in American high schools.

Nerds are the academic achievers and are seen as not being as socially adept. Nerds often keep a low profile as to their academic ability since being too smart in high school is often seen as not being cool.

Violence

Ten percent of all public schools had violent incidents. Most of the violence is done by students against other students.

Graduating from High School

Exit Exams
Twenty-two of the 50 states have exit exams to pass before you get a high school diploma. Students who do not pass the test may retake it many times.

Community Service
Some states require that students perform volunteer work before they graduate.

"It looks good on the application."
Many American students volunteer in an organization because college admission officials consider these non-academic activities important on a student's application.

American schools. Academic subjects compete for students' time to participate in team sports, extra-curricular activities, and part-time work after school. Since students are admitted into college based on academics and social development, these activities are taken very seriously.

Which group do you belong to? Peer pressure puts you into groups depending on the balance between academics or sports. *Nerds* are students who study all the time and get good grades. *Jocks* are students on the football or basketball team. As Americans value athletes, the jocks are usually the most popular students in the school. You can be both, of course, a serious student and a member of the basketball team, but there is so much pressure to belong to one group in high school, students usually spend their time with one circle of friends.

The most cheerful, peppy, and energetic people you could ever see are high-school cheerleaders. They try out to become a member of the squad just like a sports team. Dressed in sparkling uniforms and waving pom poms, cheerleaders stand in a line and yell phrases or cheers to encourage their team to win. They also kneel and stand on top of each other like pyramids, do cartwheels and amazing acrobatics. Cheerleaders are very entertaining to fans who have come to watch the game.

Compared to Asian countries, where students go to school all day long, American schools look like social centers. After finishing their high school day in the afternoon, many students in Japan and Korea attend tutoring schools and return home to their parents late at night.

The emphasis on sports or other activities in American high schools has led to students graduating with various levels of academic ability. Many high school graduates go to college without the most basic reading and math skills. Colleges, in turn, have been forced to give remedial classes in Math and English. Recently, college officials have pressured high schools to raise their standards by requiring students to take exit exams to get a high school diploma.

Some states have recently adopted the exit exam. High schools, however, are still examining the effect that these exams have on their graduation rates. High school students begin to take the exit exam in tenth grade. The exam consists of an English portion and a math portion. Many students take the math portion of the exam several times before they pass. In the Third International Mathematics and Science Study, a study of U.S. twelfth grade student achievement in math and science in 1998, Americans ranked 19th among math students in 21 countries of the world. The senior year in high school is often dedicated to passing this exit exam. This is in addition to the standardized state tests given every two years throughout school. The number of tests that American students are taking today is dramatically increasing. Some critics believe that this excessive testing in schools is turning our high schools into test preparation institutes rather than schools of learning.

Some American high schools also require students to do community service before they graduate. This requirement is seen as a way to force students to think of others while giving back to the community. Students must work a certain number of hours in activities such as coaching basketball for younger children, reading to the blind, or tutoring elementary-school children. Businesses have also looked for students who have volunteered their time to serve others. Best Buy, an electronics chain, has even offered scholarships for students who do community service. One of their recent ads reads, "We want students with great hearts."

An alternative to either private or public schools is keeping your children home and teaching them yourself. Home schooling is legal in the United States and an estimated one million, or 2%, of children are taught this way. Home-schooled children have school-approved textbooks and guidelines, and a vast network of like-minded parents.

Parents who home-school take their children on field trips with other home-schoolers to give their children the social skills that regular schools provide.

Home schooling is on the rise because of the lower academic standards of regular schools. Many parents also choose this option for safety reasons in light of the rise in school shootings. There are other parents who are fundamentalist Christians and choose home schooling because they want to limit their children's exposure to mainstream values.

Getting into College

There is often a big leap from high school to college in the United States. Colleges are much harder, and their academic standards are higher than in high schools. Half of our high school graduates enter college but only 25% graduate. Many drop out because it's too hard, or because it costs too much.

Since the quality of high schools is hard to measure across the nation, we have one standardized admission test, the Scholastic Aptitude Test or SAT, for all colleges in the United States. You must do well on this test to get into college. Many students who get a low score on the SAT go to a community college for two years and later transfer to a four-year university. That way, their grades in the community college are counted instead of the score on the SAT.

The myth in the United States is that all people are treated equally and getting into college is just a question of merit. This is not true. It is not just a matter of what you earned by your good grades and high marks on the various standardized tests, it is more complex than that, and more highly subjective than pure merit.

Besides the SAT score, college admission officials consider the grades you received in high school, an application essay, and your extracurricular activities. Another important factor is if your Mom or Dad went to that college. Sons and daughters of alumni tend to be preferred in the selection process.

On the other hand, if you are the first in your family to go to college, this also makes a difference and weighs in your favor. Some colleges give preference to minorities under a controversial policy called "Affirmative Action."

Colleges in the United States were segregated until the 1950's. The Civil Rights Movement of the 1960's broke down some race barriers and colleges began to recruit blacks and other minorities through their Affirmative Action policies. These policies consider not only grades and activities, but race is also factored into the admission process. Some white students have claimed that they had better grades and qualifications, and yet were not admitted into the college because of the color of their skin. Some "reverse discrimination" cases have been won in court and they have motivated some colleges to eliminate their Affirmative Action policies.

One such case at the University of Michigan recently reached the Supreme Court. The highest court ruled in favor of its Affirmative Action policy. What we may see in the near future is other colleges following suit and reestablishing Affirmative Action programs that they had previously eliminated.

Paying for College

Once American young people get into college, the worry about how to pay for it really begins. Worrying about how to pay for college actually began when you were born, but now payment is required and the immediacy of the need for money sinks in.

Going to college is very expensive for families who are used to having all their public elementary, junior high and high schools free. The average college tuition with room and board for in-state students is $14,000 a year at a four-year public university. For a private four-year university, the average tuition with room and board is $34,000, but can be much higher.

Many parents pay for most of their children's college tuition. The rest is usually borrowed from the federal government in the form of student loans that have low-interest rates which vary, but are currently at around 3%. Students apply for any possible financial help. If you are one of the top students, in the top 10% of your high school, you may be able to receive a scholarship that you won't have to pay back.

Most students, however, take out student loans that they must begin paying back to the federal government a year after graduating. Some college students also hold down part-time jobs, but the money earned from a job is usually small and is used for a bit of spending money.

Despite some financial help from the government, American university students usually graduate with nearly $20,000 in debt, and still have to look for their first career-related job in a tight job market. Since finding a job in a field related to your college major is difficult, recent graduates might take any job offer within the first year after graduating. They often do this because of the pressure of having to begin repayment of their student loans. To help students with their college debt, former President Clinton started a national service program called the Americorps, where students can work in a needy neighborhood after college. By working in a public service job or in a low-income neighborhood, recent graduates can cancel all or part of their student loans. This national service program gives an alternative to students.

College Life

Half of the college students in the United States are adults 25 and over. It's not unusual to see someone your mother's age, or even your grandmother's age, sitting next to you in the college classroom and asking what the homework was from the last class. Many are working adults with families who have decided to go back to school for professional advancement. Others never finished college, but have decided to return several years later.

Many of our colleges have international students advancing their careers in their countries with an American graduate degree. While only 2% of the student body is international for undergraduate programs, at the graduate level, international students make up 20% of our master's programs and 30% of our doctoral degrees. Business is the most popular field of study for international students in the United States, followed by engineering, math, and computer science.

People from other countries are surprised to learn that American college students often change their majors in the course of their college years. Some students do not know what their major field of study will be, even though they are in their first or second year of college. College students can register their major as "undeclared," and still take classes in many subjects. When asked what they will do with their degree after graduating from college, a great number of college students say they do not know beyond "look for a job."

Fraternities and Sororities

On American college campuses, the land of alleged equality, we have peculiar social clubs that cost a lot of money to join, called fraternities and sororities. Fraternities are exclusive all male clubs, and sororities are all female clubs. They are more than just clubs, however, these groups rent houses and live together and do most of their social activities together. You can see their presence in the Greek letters that identify these groups such as *Sigma Alpha Epsilon* and *Alpha Delta Phi*.

At the beginning of each semester or quarter, fraternities and sororities recruit new members through a process called rush week. They host a series of parties at the houses where they invite potential club members to get to know the current members.

The purpose of these clubs is to meet somebody of your own social class, namely, upper middle class or upper class, instead of possibly choosing your life partner from a much bigger social circle. Exclusivity is the key issue here because these clubs have annual dues that students must pay. Fraternities and sororities also charge students a membership fee, which could be from hundreds to thousands of dollars a year to join, depending on the fraternity or sorority you choose.

These clubs are well-known for their beer-drinking parties. They order kegs, turn the music up loud, and often party inside and outside of their fraternity or sorority houses. They are a very noticeable presence on college campuses, and in the surrounding neighborhoods if they live off-campus. Some of these houses have caused enough problems that neighbors have complained and colleges have put restrictions on them. Some fraternities and sororities have even been banned entirely from college campuses.

In addition to the sorority and fraternity clubs found on American college campuses, sports take on a new importance in college. Sports teams bring in money, and athletes are often recruited for their ability on the field, not in the classroom. Many adults watch college sports on television and the teams are big moneymakers for the university. This may be why universities have made academic exceptions for athletes. Alumni, or former graduates of a university, are big contributors to colleges when they have a winning football team. This, in turn, allows colleges to offer athletes a generous "benefits package" and sends a message to young adults that athletes are highly valued in our society.

American houses are bigger but our families are smaller...

2000
2200 square feet
(204 square meters)
Family size: 2.6

1970
1,500 square feet
(139 square meters)
Family size: 3

1950
1,000 square feet
(93 square meters)
Family size: 3.4

Source: U.S. Census Bureau & National Association of Home Builders

Chapter 10:

A House for Display

Visitors to the United States are often surprised to see that American houses are often single family detached homes. Our housing developed this way with a population density so low that we could afford the space. There are 70 people per square mile (29 people per square kilometer) compared to Japan's density of 880 people per square mile (340 people per square kilometer), reports the United Nations in 2001.

Many multi-levels houses or apartments in urban areas of the United States are known as "projects" rather than high-rises because they are often reserved for low-income families who receive government assistance. Public housing is usually located in the downtown areas of cities, and it suffers from a bad reputation as a place of criminal activity.

Other foreign visitors comment on how plain our houses are. Unlike Europe, we live in homes with few architectural details or ornamentation, especially if built after World War II. Few cathedrals exist in the United States, and the only castle is in Disneyland.

Most American homes are single-family detached houses and cheaply built. We commonly use wood because we used to have abundant forests that provided us with lumber. Even if it's a highly flammable building material compared to brick, stone or concrete, wood is still used because it is inexpensive. For the West Coast, wood is also a lighter construction material in the case of an earthquake.

The East Coast and Midwest regions have sturdier houses made of brick, stone and concrete and often have a basement for the tornadoes or hurricanes possible in those areas. Building materials also need to be stronger and more insulated for the colder climates.

The Southwest has little rain so we see flat-roofed houses. Unlike countries in Latin America with similar climates, Americans do not make the roof of the house sturdy enough to use as a patio. We would need to invest in cement frames and posts, which would mean more expensive materials. That kind of cement construction in the United States is generally reserved for public buildings.

Today, new American homes have walls and floors made of drywall and plywood about an inch (25 cm) thick. If you live in an apartment complex, the sounds of your neighbors travel through the walls and make for little privacy. You hear neighbors' footsteps and flushing toilets, too.

It's a bit unusual that Americans love privacy, but their homes usually have a huge window facing the street in order to view the world from the inside. People passing by on the street can also peer in from the outside and see what is going on inside the house. Americans like privacy, but that implies privacy in the family. The sense of privacy among strangers isn't as strong.

Most American houses are not fenced or gated so the home's entrance is not protected at all. In some neighborhoods, the front door of the house is only steps away from the street. Compared to other countries that have heavily gated entrances, such as Brazil, it seems most Americans blindly trust that burglars won't break into their homes, or gangs won't ruin the exterior of their homes.

Our nation is a little more than 200 years old, and therefore American houses are often built to conform to housing styles from Europe. We use every period time imaginable; Victorian, Queen Anne's, or Tudor just to name a few.

Today, new houses are built like Hollywood movie sets. Real estate developers plan communities with identical houses and a certain time period and style. The wooden frame is put up practically overnight. A facade of plaster an inch thick covers the thin walls and now you have a cheap replica of a 15th century Mediterranean, or you can go back to the Middle Ages with a Tudor style, imitate a Spanish mission, or a Western ranch.

Who cares if there are no palm trees naturally growing in your region of the country? If you want to project a tropical paradise, a retail store of exotic plants is around the corner. Palm trees can be imported from thousands of miles away and planted to give your property an authentic twist.

Sixty-seven percent of Americans own their homes. We have mobile homes that provide an affordable home to many people who otherwise wouldn't be able to own a home. These houses on wheels are the modern-day equivalent of covered wagons. Owners of the mobile homes usually take off the wheels and park their homes in a rented space in a mobile park. Mobile parks operate like a regular neighborhood, though major storms and tornadoes have been known to sweep through and destroy entire mobile home parks in the United States.

Americans feel nostalgic for their rural roots. The frontier has remained with us. The vast open spaces of the prairie can be seen in the front and back of American homes. Today, they are called front and back yards. They are mowed and trimmed just to sit there like "Little Houses on the Prairie."

Garages

There are 65 million garages in the U.S. and demand for bigger ones is growing.

Three-car Garages

18% of American homes have three-car garages, but only 13% of Americans parked three cars in their garages.

Using Garages For Storage

We fill them with wheelbarrows, camping gear, bicycles, a workbench, another refrigerator, a lawn mower and gardening tools.

Front and Back Yards

Having nicely mowed lawns is a symbol of status among neighbors in the United States. The lawn tradition was transplanted to the United States from England.

○ **Front Yards** – During most of the year, the front yard must be finely trimmed with edges clearly cut. In the winter, how you decorate your house for the holidays is also a sign of status when lawns can no longer be displayed.

○ **Back Yards** – Back yards (and sometimes front yards) are sometimes filled with play structures for kids, a pool, a deck and a grill for barbecues in the summer.

○ **"Not in my back yard,"** is an American expression for anywhere but here. When communities want to open a drug rehabilitation, recycling center or low-income housing, sometimes neighbors organize and protest having these places in their neighborhood.

Some Americans plant vegetable and flower gardens, but most importantly, they carefully maintain their lawns. To an outsider, these unused lawns seem to be a waste of space. But to an American, they fulfill the longing for open space and the feeling of "being free." Unused spaces seem to contradict the notion that Americans are practical people. These ideas of space may be on an unconscious level to most Americans. When asked about their expansive lawns, many just want to have a piece of land so others can admire it.

While houses have grown larger in the suburbs, families have shrunk. The average size home in the United States is 2,200 square feet (204 square meters), according to the National Association of Home Builders, in its 2008 report. In 1970, the average new single home being built was 1,500 square feet (139 square meters). At the same time, the average family has gone from an average of two or three children a generation ago to couples having one or two children with many families remaining childless.

We have so much space that we don't even realize it. To put our roominess in perspective, compare the square meters or footage to a sampling of countries around the world, based on Peter Menzel's book, *Material World.*

In Japan, the average size house, 1421 sq. ft. (132 square meters). Size of household: 4 people. Living room, dining room, kitchen, and bath. Traditionally, Japan has used one room for many purposes: to eat meals, socialize and to sleep. After meals, the dining table was put away and then mats were laid down to sleep on the floor. Today, many young Japanese have the Western style of bed, which is often put in the corner of the multi-purpose room similar to a studio apartment here in the United States.

In Brazil, the average size house is 1,100 sq. feet. (102 square meters). Size of household: 6 people. Two bedrooms, living room, kitchen, bathroom.

In Italy, 1292 sq. ft. (120 sq. meters). Size of household:

3 people. Five rooms and a garage.

In China, 600 square feet (55 square meters). Size of household: 9 people. Kitchen, living room, 3 bedrooms, 5 storage rooms.

Why do Americans want such a big home? Many Americans subconsciously view their house as a museum. They buy a big home, decorate it with expensive furniture, plaster their walls with family photos, and sometimes fill their house up with one or two children. They are busy working to pay the mortgage on this monster of a house. They only live in the house a handful of hours on Saturday and Sunday, besides sleeping there, of course.

While many Americans love a big kitchen, not that many of us cook in it. It's on exhibit too. We put in all new wooden cabinets to match the counter, stainless steel sinks, a built-in microwave and we wait for the day people come in and admire it and compliment the owners on a job well done.

Inside the house, it is common for the living room and the bedrooms not to have an overhead light fixture. You must buy lamps to light up your rooms. The dim lights of a lamp might seem like cozy candlelight compared to the bright florescent lights of Korean and Japanese homes.

A typical American house has an ice maker built into the refrigerator, a garbage disposal in the sink, air conditioners that are often set at frostbite temperatures, central heating that can be set so high as to interfere with normal breathing, and a basement that is seldom used. Opening windows is becoming rare, as we prefer the artificial air. Indoor carpeting is common in living rooms and bedrooms, and we seldom take off our shoes when entering our homes. Americans who buy white carpets, status symbols in the United States, may have the rule of taking off their shoes, but this is strictly for practical reasons.

Allergies are a fairly common ailment in the United States and some people claim that it is due to the strong custom of having carpeting, which collects dust, along with the habit of using artificial air in our houses.

The refrigerator, in particular, has taken on a strange role in American culture. This oversized box not only stores our food but also serves as a family communication center.

Used as a bulletin board, it is decorated with photos, children's artwork, grocery lists, messages, memos, calendars and just about anything else to remind us how proud or how busy we are as a family.

Many international students refuse to dry their clothes in American dryers. They claim that these machines are so powerful they can turn clothes into garments with loose threads or a size smaller. Hanging our clothes to drip dry in the bathroom may take quite a while to dry, but it is an option to putting clothes in the dryer, as few people in the United States use clotheslines.

Americans are reluctant to hang laundry out the window, backyard, or patio as in other countries. This could be because Americans like the convenience of having a dryer. Yet we have garage sales. Once or twice a year we empty our cluttered houses and spread our clothes out on the front yard. Aren't we ashamed of showing our personal belongings to the neighbors and asking them to buy our junk? No, the notion of making money off our belongings seems to outweigh any embarrassment for this weekend event.

Another American paradox is that we often worry about saving money in our own home and yet freely spend on the home, too. We turn off the lights to save on the electric bill. We turn down the temperature of our water heaters and take short showers so the water bill is low. At the same time, we set a timer to water the grass every day. The sprinkler waters the grass even if it has rained on a particular day. In warm weather, we turn on the air conditioner to frigid temperatures.

For the Japanese and some European visitors, the bathrooms of the United States seem impractical. We have the bathtub, toilet, and sink all in the same room while in Japan, these rooms are all separate, so one person can use the sink or the toilet while another person is in the bathtub.

The majority of Americans take a quick shower before work. This daily ritual is seen as a means to get clean in the quickest way possible, which is unlike the ritual in Japan, where a bath is seen as a place to take your time and relax, and bathing even has a spiritual side. Americans seldom take time to relax this way, as bathing is not often viewed as a spiritual experience.

When Americans invite friends over, they clean the house and get it ready to be displayed. It is a major occasion. The house will be on exhibit. When the guests arrive, we show them around the house, (the viewing), and endlessly talk about our remodeling projects (exhibit in progress). Americans expect visitors to compliment them on the furnishings of the house or something hanging on their walls (the reception).

At the same time we have made our houses into museums, American art and science museums offer children the opportunity to stay overnight at the museum. American parents are willing to pay top dollar for their children to be educated in a museum while enjoying an overnighter with other children. The irony is found in a culture where houses are museums and museums are houses.

This notion of improving the house that you just bought is an American trait. Why aren't we satisfied with what we just bought? We always think change is better; we can always improve our house and ourselves.

Even when we have money to hire outside contractors, many of us will remodel our own homes ourselves. We go to the giant furniture and hardware stores full of prefabricated and packaged walls, windows, cabinets, lights, and furniture. By following the instructions included in the package, we assemble cabinets and install bathroom fixtures with minimal skills and tools.

This trend for remodeling your home is very popular abroad too. In the United States, we have Martha Stewart, the home decorating guru, to help us. Though Martha Stewart was found guilty of lying about a stock-trading deal and was sentenced to five months in prison in July of 2004, Stewart plans to continue giving out recipes and entertaining ideas to her American followers. While we have Martha Stewart to tell us how to decorate our interior in the United States, in other countries, they have their own queens of interior design helping them remake their homes.

Air Conditioning

Why are Americans so in love with air conditioning? Cool artificial air has become such an essential part of American culture that people from outside the United States often comment on it. Americans mostly see air conditioning as positive and necessary while many international visitors might view it as a luxury and point to it as a wasteful aspect of our culture. In general, windows in office buildings have been sealed shut because of the central air conditioning.

In its early years, air conditioning was seen as a luxury in the U.S. It was mainly used in department stores, movie theaters and rail cars. But after World War II, air conditioning entered the home of the average American. Since then, air conditioning has changed what we do in our leisure time. Before houses were air-conditioned, people used to sit on their front porches and chat with neighbors to get away from the heat of their houses. Or they would go out to an air-conditioned public place. Today, air conditioning has encouraged families to stay indoors in the summer months. We go outdoors less often and instead, choose indoor activities such as watching television. In addition, the United States went through a huge population shift from the Northern cities to the Sunbelt cities of Houston, Phoenix, Las Vegas, and Miami with the widespread use of air conditioning.

The Homeless

First-time visitors to the United States are amazed at the number of homeless we have in this country. This reflects that the gap between the rich and the poor is getting wider in this country.

In the United States, people who are poor hold up a sign instead of extending their hand. They stand on a corner all day with a piece of cardboard, and on it is usually written, "Homeless, please help," or "Will work for food." They beg during daylight, and some return to a house at night. Some of these people are not homeless at all, but they are most likely jobless. Others, however, are truly homeless, and rummage through garbage dumpsters for cans and bottles at night or in early morning hours.

Those who are homeless and sleeping on the streets can usually be identified by their tattered clothes, blankets, and shopping cart full of discards. We do have shelters for them in our large cities, but not nearly enough. The shelters have curfews and rules about alcohol and drugs. Many of the homeless have addiction problems that forbid them to use the shelters.

People living in poverty make up roughly 14% of our population and finding affordable housing is a challenge. Many of the poor struggle to pay rent with their low-wage jobs and declining government assistance. For people having difficulty paying the rent, a serious illness or disability can cause them to be homeless.

Though many international visitors wonder how many homeless there are, the number of homeless people is very difficult to measure because homelessness is frequently a temporary circumstance and not a permanent one.

Notes

"A man builds a house in England with the expectation of living in it and leaving it to his children; we shed our houses in America as easily as a snail does his shell."

— Harriet Beecher Stowe, American author (1811-1896)

Diverse Religions

The Mormons *(also known as The Latter-day Saints)*

○ Thirteen million members in more than 150 countries and territories. About 5.5 million live in the U.S.

○ Founder Joseph Smith, religious book: *The Book of Mormon.*

○ **Live a disciplined life** – No coffee, tea, cigarettes, alcohol or premarital sex.

○ **Baptism of the dead** – Because of the belief of baptism of their ancestors, the tracing of one's family tree has become very important to the Mormons. This religion holds one of the best genealogical archives in the U.S.

○ **Two-year missionary service** – For single young men (19 years old) or retired couples. They travel in pairs. One and a half year missionary assignment for single females (21 years old).

The Christian Scientists *(The Church of Christ)*

○ 200,000 members, based in Boston, Mass.

○ Founder Mary Baker Eddy, 1879, religious text: *Science and Health.*

○ **Refuse medical treatment** and rely on faith healing by Christian Science practitioners. Claims of miraculous healing.

The Amish *(also known as "The Plain People")*

○ 144,000 members, founder Jacob Amman.

○ Emigrated from Europe as farmers in the 1700s and 1800s, mainly live in the rural Midwest today.

○ **Reject modern conveniences** such as electricity, cars, air travel, jewelry and divorce.

○ **Amish families have an average of seven children**. Almost 25% have ten or more children.

○ **Follow *Ordnung* rules**: Wear dark clothing, marry other Amish, and will not serve in the military.

Chapter 11:

God & Good Luck

W hy are people so religious in the United States? We talk about God all the time in our political and legal institutions. The president ends his political speeches with, *"God bless America."* The U.S. Congress starts with a prayer before it begins its session. American children stand up at the beginning of their school day reciting "The Pledge of Allegiance" while promising to be loyal to *". . . one nation, under God."* Our coins say, *"In God we trust."* If you are a witness in a trial, you take an oath: "Do you swear to tell the whole truth and nothing but the truth, *so help you God?"*

Is this the same country that proclaims the separation of church and state? What you see are many references to God because the overwhelming majority believe in a God. In a recent Harris Poll, Americans were surveyed about their religious beliefs and 90% of Americans said they believed in God, but *less than half* of the population actually practice religious rituals by going to a church on a regular basis.

While Americans have limited choice for presidential and congressional candidates, with only two major political parties, the number of religious groups is extensive. Protestants alone count over 300 denominations, according to Barry A. Kosmin and Seymour P. Lachman in *One Nation Under God*, a book that presents the results of an extensive 1990 national survey in which 100,000 Americans were asked to identify their religion.

Who are the religious in America?

Fifty-two percent of American adults are Protestant, 24.5% are Catholic and 14.1% adhere to no religion, reports *The American Religious Identification Survey 2001*, an in-depth survey asking Americans about their religion. This 2001 survey was done by City University of New York as a follow-up to the extensive *One Nation Under God* 1990 survey.

As you can see, about 77% of Americans claim Christianity as their religion. Christianity is on the decline, however, in the United States. The 2001 survey revealed the number of Americans who claim to be Christians went from 86% only ten years ago to the current 77%. Over the same ten-year period, Americans who were not affiliated with any religion jumped from 8% to 14%.

Still, Christianity continues to dominate the fabric of our society. Religious diversity in the United States is Christian diversity. Considering our ethnic diversity, a surprising number of people in this country have a similar outlook about religion.

Americans ranked first in a 1989 Gallup International survey asking young adults 18 to 24 the importance of religion. Ninety percent of American young adults said it was important, compared to young Brazilians (80%), Koreans (68%), Japanese (38%) and Chinese (4%).

While most Americans agree on the basic Christian beliefs, they vary widely on the organized practice of their religion.

On one hand, you have people who attend Church

on an occasional basis, for baptisms, funerals and at Christmas and Easter. Their Bible probably is collecting dust on the bedroom nightstand. These are Christians who don't participate in the organized part of religion and see their faith as a largely private matter between God and themselves.

On the other hand, you have the fundamentalists and evangelical Christians, most heavily in the Southern states, who make up the 20% of Christians who are considered extremely religious. They are the "born again" Christians who are on a mission to convert the rest of the world to Christianity. Many of these fundamentalists are ardent churchgoers who go to church more than once a week, read their Bible on a daily basis and interpret the Bible literally. They don't smoke, drink, or dance. Southern Baptists are by far the largest majority of fundamentalists in the United States, making up one third of the Protestants.

This religious divide between those who pay lip service to their Church versus the active, practicing Christians in the United States polarizes Americans more than the differences between Catholics and Protestants.

Some active church members give to churches because this donation is tax deductible. This can reduce the amount of money Americans pay to the state and federal government at tax time. If there is one thing Americans hate it is paying taxes. A popular adage in the United States says, "There are only two things you must do in the United States, die and pay taxes."

Most Americans think Christianity is exclusive. You can't believe in Christianity and another religion at the same time. This concept differs in other countries, where they borrow religious rites and believe that different religions can be practiced alongside one another.

In Japan, for example, people practice rituals from different religions at different stages of their life. When a baby is born, the Japanese go to a shrine to pray to the native gods. At certain ages, 3, 5 and 7, the Japanese also go to a shrine to celebrate their children's birthdays in the Shinto style. In a wedding ceremony, many go to a church and exchange marriage vows in front of Christ. Then it is a common Japanese practice to bury the dead in a Buddhist ceremony. This type of practicing various religious rites at different times in your life is unheard of in the United States.

Many immigrants change their religion when they come to the United States. Those who were not religious in their native countries arrive here and may join a religion out of sheer loneliness and the overwhelming feeling of being an outsider to the mainstream culture.

When Korean immigrants come to the United States, many of them join a Christian church, though Koreans have traditionally come from a Buddhist country. Korean immigrants often become active in churches here to feel a part of a community that often substitutes for the family unit they miss in their countries. Some have changed because of the social aspects of Christianity compared to Buddhism's more personal view. Also, there are few Buddhists temples in the United States.

Hispanic immigrants often change their religion in the United States too. Latin America is predominantly Catholic, but in the United States, Hispanics who become Protestants tend to gravitate toward the Evangelicals and Pentecostals. The Protestant faiths recruit new members with strong missionary activities compared to the Catholic denomination. They also offer social services and access to government services, which the Catholics also offer, but to a lesser degree. Some of these Protestant churches even sponsor the newly-arrived immigrants. If immigrants work three years as religious workers for the church, the church may help them get their permanent legal residence.

Some churches cater to the new immigrant and are called ethnic churches. They offer English language classes, job and housing assistance as well as serving immigrants' spiritual needs.

The government typically provides these kinds of

services to Americans. In the case of immigrants, however, it is frequently the church that helps them to adjust to a new life in the United States. Moreover, the church gives them practical information and a social network of people who speak their own language.

Religion in the United States is less based on ethnic history, like Hinduism, Buddhism, and Muslim faiths, and more based on personal choice. Americans choose their denomination in the Christian faith and see nothing wrong with changing churches. You can go to a Methodist church service this Sunday and then a Lutheran service the next. You can officially change from Catholic to Pentecostal if you want to take some classes.

Americans may believe in many things that their organized religion might not follow. They see nothing wrong with this. For example, the Catholic Church is against abortion and divorce, but many Catholics believe these are personal issues and disagree with Church teaching. On the issue of abortion, Americans who believe in the right to have an abortion are not called supporters of abortion but *pro choice*.

How old you are may also determine your church attendance. American children usually follow their parents to church, as the parents want to pass on the moral principles of their religion to their children. This church attendance may drop off during the teen years. As adults age, attendance at religious services rises again. Seniors make up a large number of the faithful in churches. Could this reflect the fact that many seniors live alone, and may be one of the loneliest groups of people in American society?

Going to Catholic churches in the United States differs from the churches in other Catholic countries. In Latin American countries, the Catholic Church usually is very ornate and people come to pray silently and intensely for loved ones, often clutching a photograph or rosary.

Here, going to Church is very informal. Some people wear jeans, come to Mass late, and bring crayons and coloring books to keep their child occupied for an hour. All of this makes the religious ritual resemble more of a social gathering than a religious ceremony.

We shake hands with the usher when we go into church. Then during the Mass, we offer each other the sign of peace, shaking hands with people around us and wishing them peace. We recite the Lord's Prayer, holding hands with the person in our pew. We clap at the end of Mass to show the appreciation to the organist who plays the music.

As we go out the door, we greet the priest at the bottom of the steps where he waits to shake hands with us, and we thank him for the sermon. After mass, most people meet in the church hall for coffee and doughnuts to socialize some more. In the United States, with three handshakes and one round of applause, the mass is less a spiritual ritual than a "feel happy" pageant where people are the performers.

Christianity is so strong in the United States that the Muslims, Jews, Buddhists, and Hindus take a back seat in the religious spectrum. Americans have varying degrees of tolerance for other religions. In the past, we had freedom of religion as long as it was our religion. Native Americans were practicing their own tribal religions when the colonists arrived. Then these unknown and frightening religions were forbidden. Native Americans were not allowed to practice their religious ceremonies and publicly pray to their gods again until 1978, when the federal government passed the American Indian Religious Freedom Act.

Black slaves had their African tribal religions when they arrived, but were forced to convert to Christianity. This forced conversion worked against the white man in the long run. It indirectly helped eliminate slavery, as religion became a spiritual fountain for slaves hoping for freedom. Churches also turned out to be the places to politically organize against the white man in the segregated South.

When we see Muslim women covered with a headscarf or Jewish men with a cap, some Americans tend to feel uncomfortable. If two Christians are carrying around a Bible, however, few Americans are surprised. We are accustomed to seeing missionaries on street corners. Still, when any religious minority shows something public, such as dressing in religious garb, it makes many Americans nervous because of a belief that religion should be private, not public.

Americans tend to overestimate the size of minority religions in the United States, which account for only 4% of the population. The most visible minority religions are from the Jewish and Muslim faiths. Though Jews make up only 1.3% of our religious population and Muslims 0.5%, their religious dress and holidays often identify these religious minorities and makes them a target of prejudice.

New York is the home to more Jews (25%) and Muslims (24%) than any other state. In New York City, for example, public schools have the major Jewish holidays off. In schools throughout the United States, however, school officials have been challenged to accommodate religious minorities. This means schools have had to excuse students' absences for religious holidays or find a place for Muslim students to go to at lunchtime during the month of Ramadan, when Muslim students fast.

The term Arab is an ethnic category, and Islam is a religion. Not all Arabs are Muslims and not all Muslims are Arabs. Most Americans confuse Arabs with Muslims and think they are the same. This is a myth based on the lack of knowledge of cultures other than our own.

In fact, the majority of Arabs in the United States are not Muslims. Arab Christians such as Egyptian Copts, Lebanese Maronites and Iraqi Chaldeans have made their home here.

The Muslim faith is growing fast in the United States because of the large numbers of African Americans who convert to Islam today.

We have had anti-Catholic incidents in the past, but today anti-Semitic and anti-Muslim sentiments prevail with a rise in hate crimes directed toward Jews and Muslims. In the year 2007, the FBI reported 967 hate crimes against Jews and 156 against Muslims in its Uniform Crime Reports.

Secular groups, the 14% who don't claim any religion, include humanists, secularists, and atheists. They have been instrumental in keeping Christian practices out of schools.

Madalyn Murray, a Texas atheist, challenged Bible reading and prayers in public schools. She fought against a 1963 mandatory Bible reading law in Pennsylvania schools, and the case reached the Supreme Court. She also challenged saying the "Our Father" prayer in Maryland public schools. The Supreme Court ruled on these cases together and banned government-sponsored religious activities in public schools since.

Other battles are still being fought in the courts to keep religion out of schools and courthouses. In 2003, after two years of controversy and $1 million dollars in lawyer's fees, the Alabama Courthouse had to remove a monument that was inscribed with the Ten Commandments.

The fight between religion and state continues around the world. In France, a law was recently enacted which bans head scarves for Muslim girls, skullcaps for Jewish boys and large crosses for Christians.

Good Luck

When Americans cannot figure out why something happened, which they constantly try to do, they resort to talking about good luck and bad luck. Luck is more socially acceptable to talk about than beliefs in God, though we talk about both.

Some of us become jealous when we see other people doing well. We dismiss the success of others and say, "They were lucky." Or if something bad happens to people who we think did not deserve the misfortune, we say the opposite, " It was a case of bad luck."

If we interpret success and misfortune in religious terms, it would sound something like this for misfortune, "It was meant to be," or for success, "My prayers were answered." You hear these expressions in the United States, too. By observing what Americans say when told of good and bad news, you can often gauge how religious they are.

Good luck in the United States is a very general, catch-all term to wish someone well in whatever he undertakes. In fact, it is a common way of saying good-bye when we know a person has to take a test, apply for a job, or get out of a troublesome predicament.

I *lucked out* means I was lucky. The luck of the Irish means you were very lucky, though you don't have to be Irish to claim this special status. Many Americans wear a special piece of jewelry for luck, and wearing good luck charms is as common as seeing Christian crosses. You can spot these good luck charms hanging from the rear view window of many cars. There is even a popular cold cereal called Lucky Charms.

In some countries, people don't use the words good luck as often as we do. In the Korean language, words for wishing good luck are usually tied to a particular event. For example, when you take a test, there is a special word to do well on the test that would be equivalent to the American general "good luck." When a baby is born, there is another kind of good luck word. For ritual moments and everyday situations, the word changes and is tied to the action. In English, our vocabulary isn't as rich to express the nuances of the event. The most you could do to tie it to an event is say, "Good luck on your test."

Americans knock on wood three times when they say good things about themselves. This is to prevent bad things from happening by telling others of our successes. This practice dates back to pre-Christian times when we believed trees had good and bad spirits inside. By knocking on them, the evil spirits would be driven away.

Some Americans also believe in astrology and may ask you, "What's your sign?" The Western horoscope is based on your birthday and divided into 12 astrological signs with a whole set of personality characteristics for each sign. Some people believe that if you know the hour and the exact date you were born, a person shares personality traits with other people born with similar planetary experiences.

"Are you Aquarius? You must be friendly. Libras and Aquarians get along." While some Americans just follow astrology for fun, others really believe in it as a kind of prediction.

Americans rarely know our blood type unless we have had a medical problem and our doctors have told us. This often surprises international people, especially the Japanese. The Japanese not only ask each other about their blood types, but some even want to match the compatibility of their blood type to a potential mate.

In Chinese and Korean cultures, people often go to a fortune teller to determine the best date on the calendar to get married. Americans do not have this idea that certain days are considered lucky days to get married or to make major business decisions. The closest equivalent would be the daily horoscope column in newspapers.

Good luck and bad luck numbers vary in cultures, too. In China, the numbers 6 and 8 are considered good luck numbers. In Chinese, 6 means smoothly and 8 means fortune. If you put 6 and 8 together, it roughly means good fortune.

We consider the number 13 as unlucky in the United States, as do many Western European and Latin American countries. Skyscrapers are built without the 13th floor. However, the number 4 is considered unlucky in Japan, Korea and China because the pronunciation of this word sounds similar to the word "death." Many people in these countries do not want cell phone numbers with the number 4 in them.

Notes

"We are all tattooed in our cradles with the beliefs of our tribe."

– Oliver Wendell Holmes, Sr.
American author and physician (1809-1904)

Cities That Restrict Cars to Reduce Traffic

Rome, Florence and Milan
These Italian cities have closed the center of their cities to cars, making them wonderful walking cities.

Mexico City
This city has closed the downtown Zocalo area to automobiles.

London
Drivers must pay to enter the center of the city.

Hong Kong
Drivers must pay to enter the city.

Singapore
Drivers of cars with fewer than four people pay a monthly fee if they enter the city during the morning rush hour.

Tokyo
Car owners must show government officials that they have rented a parking space or car port before they are able to register their cars.

Chapter 12:

A Colony of Cars

W hat do Americans do in cars? Roll down your window and take a look. We put on make-up, undress and dress ourselves, drink hot coffee, pick our nose, read the newspaper and work from our cell phones. We seem to think because a metal bubble encases us, our private life is invisible.

We even party in parking lots, which we call a "tailgate party." Before a football game, we open our trunks packed with beer and sandwiches, unfold chairs and sit in the parking lot with friends to get in the mood to see a football game.

Our cars talk. What we wish to stand up for and say in person, we stick on our cars. Bumper stickers and license plate frames reveal our deepest feelings and political beliefs. There must be a great number of proud parents in this country because one of the most common bumper stickers is, "My child is an honor student at Jefferson Elementary School." The second most common sticker is when that child is all grown up and now shows off what college he graduated from by displaying a sticker that says, "Alumni of New York University."

Then there are the bumper stickers that tell us where we would like to be, "I'd rather be shopping." Others show how much we love our cats and dogs, how sexy we are, and what non-profit organizations we are members of.

The car is so much a part of the American psyche that a driver's license functions as a national identity card in the United States. "Carding you" is another way to ask for our identification when we buy alcohol or cigarettes. Everyone is supposed to have one. Even if you don't drive, you get the same card as a driver. The only difference is that the card is used for identity purposes instead of driving. Police officers, of course, use your driver's license number when they stop you for traffic violations. By entering your number, they can access all kinds of personal information on the computer installed in the police car. Besides the ownership and registration of the car, your driving record and previous home addresses can be accessed in minutes.

Some Americans who can't afford a house invest in a beautiful car instead. It is a status symbol. They install stereo equipment and CD players in their BMWs or convertibles and cruise around with the volume turned up and the sound of the car vibrates for blocks.

Americans feel more powerful in their cars. When we get mad at a driver in heavy traffic, we are ruder and more aggressive than if we were face to face. This aggressive behavior is called "road rage." We hang our heads out of the window or get close enough to the other car so we can curse at them. A few people even try to side-swipe your car. Other people get out of their cars in heavy traffic or at a stoplight and start yelling at a driver who had failed to use turn signals or had cut in front of a car.

Though the Toyota Camry and the Honda Civic have been competing for the best-selling car title in the last couple of decades, many of us prefer to drive big cars like

Sport Utility Vehicles, commonly known as SUVs.

Why do we drive so many big cars and trucks? We feel like kings of the road. We like to see above other cars and we want the comfort of the space, since we spend an enormous amount of time in our cars. Americans drive an average of two hours a day just going back and forth to work. This does not include the time spent in our cars doing errands and dropping off and picking up our children. We live in our cars.

Do Americans even consider gas mileage? For many people, the power and comfort that comes with space is considered more important than the mileage and the cost of gasoline. As long as gas is cheaper than most of the world pays, we'll keep buying SUVs and other gas-guzzlers.

Cars have made walking around in the city mostly obsolete in the United States. Most Americans dislike walking as a means for transport. In Europe, people make between 25-40% percent of their trips by foot or bicycle in suburbs, compared to just 7 percent of Americans' trips. Walking is seen as a hardship or a sign of poverty. It is only socially acceptable when it looks like an organized sport and it looks sweaty. Proper exercise shorts, a sleeveless T-shirt, an iPod, and sports shoes are needed. A fast, hard stride makes us look like serious walkers. In the United States, we like to say, "I took a *power walk*." With our arms swinging back and forth and our feet pounding the cement, we look straight ahead and count how many blocks we've walked and how many calories we are burning off.

Our refusal to see walking as a pleasurable means of getting somewhere even applies to short trips around the neighborhood. Why should we walk when we have driveways next to our houses? Many Americans even drive a short walking distance to places in our neighborhoods such as banks, the dry cleaners and the post office. The convenience of having drive-through fast food restaurants,

Cities Noted for Car Alternatives

○ **Curitiba, Brazil** – Has a unique bus system. Buses run on dedicated streets and provide excellent, low-cost service.

○ **Basel, Switzerland** – This city is heavily dependent on an excellent tram system and parts of the town are car-free.

○ **Groningen, Netherlands** – This European city promotes bikes as a practical means of transportation. The Netherlands also leads the world in the number of bicycle paths.

○ **Tokyo, Japan** – Fast trains replace cars in most of Tokyo.

Europe's Most Dangerous Drivers
Although Italy has a reputation for bad drivers, the worst drivers were surprisingly found in the UK in a five-country survey.

The countries polled in the International Road Traffic and Accident survey were: the UK, Germany, Italy, Spain and France.

banks and camera shops in neighborhoods discourages walking, too.

The dislike for walking can also be seen in these parking lots, where people can be quite aggressive over a parking spot. Many Americans will drive around and around a parking lot for several minutes in order to find the closest space possible so they don't have to walk so far. For people who are willing to pay for valet parking, parking attendants will help us out of our cars and leave us at the entrance of a shopping mall or fine restaurant.

Many Americans also choose not to walk to their destinations because streets in the United States are strictly made for the car. A great number of our roads lack marked crosswalks, pedestrian signals or bridges in order for people to cross a busy street. Streets without sidewalks force people to walk along the side of the road with high-speed traffic. In many states, it is legal to make a right turn on a red light after stopping in an intersection. This practice can cause accidents with pedestrians crossing the street.

Bicycling in the United States is not as popular as in Europe either. People of all ages bike in Europe. You see them on their way to work, school, or shopping. In contrast, bicyclists in the United States are mainly young people who bike for exercise or sport on the weekends.

Why do only a few Americans use the bike as a useful, non-polluting mode of transportation? It may be because we have a much lower density of people in the United States. Our cities and workplaces are usually far from our suburban homes, and so we have to travel longer distances to get to our destinations. In the United States, few roads have bike paths, and many Americans consider it dangerous to bike alongside busy traffic.

Our transportation modes might change if there were as many bike paths and sidewalks in the United States as there are in European countries. Bikers today have a hard time sharing the lanes with fast cars on the road, just as people who try to walk do. In such a car-oriented culture as ours, many Americans will continue to drive until we change our streets to accommodate walkers and bikers.

How Our Car Culture Began

One out of every two Americans has a car. Cars are so relatively plentiful that one in three cars in the world is owned by an American. Some of us have two or three cars parked in our garages.

How did we become such a colony of cars?

According to the 1996 documentary film *Taken for a Ride*, produced by Joe Klein and Martha Olson and shown on public television stations, when the automobile was still relatively in its infant stages in the 1920's, automaker General Motors bought many of the streetcars that were in operation. In 1922, only one American in ten owned an automobile. Nearly everyone else used the electric streetcars in urban areas, as they lived within walking distance of the streetcar line.

While Henry Ford was churning out over a million cars a day and making the car affordable to the middle class, the federal government gave huge subsidies to make roads and state highways.

Taken for a Ride reports that General Motors' president Alfred Sloan saw that if he eliminated the train market in the United States, he would create a new market for cars. Between 1936-1950, Sloan bought 100 electric streetcars in 45 cities and made the cities buy GM manufactured buses, thinking Americans would tire of the slow buses and feel the need to buy a car.

GM was successful despite the anti-trust and monopoly lawsuits brought against it. In 1949, GM and its partners were convicted of criminal conspiracy in the United States district court of Chicago and fined $5,000, but the fine failed to stop the company. The rest is history. The American driving culture was born.

The American housing industry, delayed by the Depression in the 1930's, began to build around the car after World War II. Realtors and land developers promoted and built suburbs far beyond city limits with only roads for individual transport and no mass transit links. Thus, many of our neighborhoods today are without access to services unless we have a car.

Traffic, Signs and Parking

When we talk about heavy traffic, it sounds like English as a foreign language with the slang the newscaster uses. Traffic jams are called *gridlock, stop-and-go* and *bumper-to-bumper traffic*. A *bottleneck* is when two roads merge and cause traffic congestion.

Traffic lights, arrows and signs point in different directions and seem to contradict themselves at intersections. Sometimes, you have to guess which sign to follow or else you can decide to go in the direction of the car in front of you.

On American highways, a series of signs for the same destination can make you dizzy. If you are going to the city of Great Neck, for instance, the sign reads, "Great Neck 5 miles," then, "Great Neck 4 miles," and signs continue to appear until the final, "Great Neck Exit." How many signs do we need for Great Neck?

Parking lots have spaces reserved for the handicapped, just as buses and trolleys have seating in the front. You'll be fined almost four hundred dollars if you park in the blue handicapped spot. Many seniors get a handicapped permit because they can't walk very far and need to park in the closest spots next to the store.

Since the handicapped permit gives access to the top parking spots, members of the family may use this permit also even though they are not handicapped in any way. This is why you may see very-able bodied teenagers pull up and park in a handicapped spot. While grandmother or mother might have a physical problem, they certainly don't. The police do not check who uses the permit but only look to see if the blue and white sign is clearly visible from the outside of the car.

Public Transportation

Why is the American public transportation system one of the worst in the industrialized world?

Seventy five percent of Americans drive alone to their jobs, while only 4.7 percent use public transportation and 0.4 percent bike to work. We have a crisis in intercity travel and mass transit in the United States.

Americans who live in the suburbs, according to studies, will use mass transit only when and if it is a real alternative to cars, such as trains and buses linking airports, schools, and a thorough network of public transportation.

What are the alternatives to driving in the United States?

It looks pretty grim.

How many cities even have a choice? Compared to Europe and Japan, we hardly have any trains yet alone high-speed trains. There is Amtrak, the only passenger train that offers interstate travel. Created in 1971, it is extremely expensive and serves only certain areas of the United States. Trains are practically invisible in this country, because they are mostly used for carrying freight. Trains carry 40% of the total freight, while the rest of the freight is still carried over land by heavy trucks. These trucks, competing with traffic on our highways, damage our roads and bridges. That has made us appear like the Romans; we build roads and bridges, dig them up and constantly repair them. The automakers have won the favor of the federal government, which gives massive subsidies to highways but very little funding to maintain trains or subsidize mass transit.

Only a handful of American cities have major subway systems: New York City, San Francisco, Boston, Philadelphia,

Washington D.C., Chicago, and a few other cities. Most of the cities in the Midwest, the South, and the West have no subways at all.

Buses in most of the country are incredibly slow and mainly serve the downtown areas of cities. Because of the limited areas served, buses have become the main transport of the poor and the elderly. Greyhound, the bus line that goes to other states, serves more areas and meets the need for cheap transportation. Students and immigrants are frequent Greyhound travelers, but many of its bus stations are in parts of inner cities that some people consider dangerous.

Many American cities are building light rail systems, but they are expensive to build and operate at slow speeds. They are also unable to move a lot of people in the short period of time that is needed for today's labor force.

Cities in other countries are at the forefront of alternatives to the car. In Tokyo, fast trains transport millions of people efficiently. In Brazil, the city of Curitiba has a unique bus system. Buses run on dedicated streets and provide low-cost service. In Basel, Switzerland, the city is heavily dependent on a tram system, and parts of the town are car-free. The Netherlands leads the world in the number of bicycle paths. And of course, the Italian cities of Rome, Florence, and Milan are walking cities because cars are banned in the downtown areas and the streets are completely filled with pedestrians.

Laws forcing drivers to leave their cars home by closing the centers of congested cities, or making drivers pay if they enter the downtown area, exist in various cities already. For example, London and Hong Kong are cities where drivers have to pay to enter the city.

Until Americans either build mass transit infrastructures to link people across the small towns and suburbs of the United States or force us to leave our cars at home, we will continue to be married to our cars.

The Buzz on Beauty

Hot Spots for Cosmetic Surgery

Bangkok, Thailand – Bangkok Preecha Aesthetic Institute.

Seoul, Korea – The Apkujong section of Seoul is well-known for its reasonable rates and high quality surgeons, also known as the "Plastic Surgery Street."

Brazil – Brazil has 3,200 plastic surgeons, second only to the United States with 6,100.

What Westerners Want	*What Asians Want*
slimmer bodies	wider eyes
wrinkle-free skin	longer noses
fuller breasts	slimmer cheeks

The Most Beautiful Women

The countries that have won the most Miss Universe and Miss World Titles combined: Venezuela (9 times), India (7 times), Sweden, (6 times).

Job Interviews in Korea and Japan

In Korea, because the job market is so competitive, there is a growing trend of recent graduates having cosmetic surgery to look better and therefore, have a competitive edge in their job interviews. In Japan, this happens too. It is called recruit *seikei*.

Chapter 13:

Beauty Marks

H ave your ever seen what you think is a beautiful woman walking in front of you, she turns around, and surprise! She's sixty years old with wrinkles on her face! There are sixty-year-olds walking around in twenty-year old bodies. You shouldn't assume that when people age in the United States they will turn ugly or fat and stay at home. Many seniors keep in good shape and lead active lifestyles.

For older American women, we have the euphemism of "growing old gracefully." This is considered a compliment and means you can be both beautiful and old.

The actress Katherine Hepburn was a model of aging beauty. Cosmetic companies market expensive creams to women to postpone this natural aging process. These beauty companies are now marketing to men for the first time. Beauty products geared to men were not needed in the past since there has always been a double standard about attractiveness as men and women age. Men have been valued both young and wrinkled but women have had to look young for the rest of their lives. How people view the aging process is a reflection of the values in a culture.

Who sets the beauty standards in the United States? Movie and television actresses, singers, Miss America winners and fashion models are *the beautiful people* in this culture. They are the role models that women seek to copy for their hairstyles, body structure and fashion.

Our beautiful people reveal the secret physical features Americans value. Look at the dolls sold in the United States. Barbie dolls, which came out in 1957, are still the most common dolls you see in children's bedrooms. Barbie was the first doll that wasn't an imitation of a baby. A doll that was a young woman who had big breasts and a boyfriend named Ken was revolutionary at the time.

Mirror, mirror on the wall, who is beautiful in the eyes of all? No one. There is no uniform standard of beauty in the United States, but the big-breasted blonde with fair skin and blue eyes remains a beauty ideal for many white women. Although there is pressure to conform to this mainstream concept of beauty, Asians, Hispanics and African Americans have their own ideals of beauty within their own communities.

For the Barbie doll wannabes, you have to be thin, and when you're thin, you usually don't have a big chest. You see women searching to be Barbies today in the lingerie section of department stores. Flat-chested, they scout for a padded bra or the push up Wonder Bras. If they have enough money, they are somewhere in a cosmetic surgeon's office undergoing surgery for silicone implants.

A sizeable number of American women wish to be blonde because they think men find blondes more attractive and sexier than brunettes. Where does this idea that blonde is better come from? Joanna Pitman in her book *On Blondes*, traces the origin of blonde hair as a symbol of beauty to the Greeks. She writes that the concept is more than two thousand years old and began with the Greek goddess of love, Aphrodite, who was blonde. During the Renaissance, the word "fair" became synonymous with beautiful in the English language.

Today, we export the myth that American women have blonde hair and blue eyes. Why are we so fixated on blonde hair? We are a youth-oriented culture and many people associate blonde hair with youth. Many babies are born with blonde hair but gradually their turns darker as they grow older. Over time, adults began to associate blonde hair with youth and fertility and it grew into an aesthetic and cultural preference.

When foreigners visit the United States, many are surprised to see the many hair colors American women really have.

Only 7 percent of American women colored their hair in 1950, and they did it mainly to cover up the gray with their natural color. Today, it is estimated that around 50% of American women color their hair. Coloring your hair for fashion's sake is popular with young, middle-aged, and older women today. Women no longer have to feel that the hair color must match their natural hair color as much as possible to disguise the fact that they are coloring it. Now American men are joining the ranks and coloring their hair in growing numbers.

Very few blondes in the United States are naturally blonde. Only one in every twenty blonde American adults in the United States is genuinely blonde while the others bleach their hair. The hair coloring industry makes a fortune off American women who want to be blonde because our culture gives a certain status to blondes.

Madonna is a natural brunette but attributes part of her success to turning blonde. For her *True Blue* album in 1986, she appeared on the cover for the first time as a bleached-blonde. More than 20 million copies sold worldwide compared to her as a brunette on previous albums that sold only 5 million copies. Madonna

Good-Looking American Men

American women generally like beefy men and the stakes are high. Since 1990, steroids have been banned in the United States yet an estimated one million Americans, most of them men, use steroids to build muscle mass. No longer limited to athletes and body-builders, many American men lift weights in a gym to get that muscular look.

immediately recognized the commercial value of blonde hair and it became part of her star image. "Being blonde is definitely a different state of mind," Madonna told *Rolling Stone* magazine. "I can't really put my finger on it, but the artifice of being blonde has some incredible sort of sexual connotation."

Women from other countries are not immune to wanting to be blonde. They watch blonde stars on *Sex in the City* and *Friends*, read *Cosmopolitan* and *Glamour* and aspire to the Western standard of beauty. No matter how naturally black their hair is in Japan, thousands of young women use peroxide there to become blonde. Some do it out of rebellion; others do it because they want to look more Western. In Brazil as well, many women turn blonde despite the fact that very few Brazilians are naturally blonde.

African American women judge a woman's beauty by her hair. As the major consumers of hair products in the United States, black women style their hair creatively into braids, twists and locks. They use flatirons, hot combs, curling irons, and rollers, and an assortment of gels. The fashion model Naomi Campbell and film actress Halle Berry have been beauty ideals for many African American women. Studies also have shown that African American women have a healthier attitude toward their bodies than white women, as they have a very low incidence of bulimia and anorexia.

Hispanic women usually think they are more beautiful wearing makeup. They are heavy users of lipstick, foundation, powder and eyeliner. Jennifer Lopez has been a role model for many Hispanic women. She has started her own line of perfume. The Hispanic beauty ideal is also curvier than the white woman's image. The Hispanic film, *Real Woman Have Curves*, is about this acceptance of a fuller body.

Asian Americans value skin that is the color of milk. They buy whitening creams in search of ivory skin in a jar. They slather on the sunscreen, wear visors, and carry umbrellas for royal protection from the sun. They also value being thin, which is skinnier than most other Americans aspire to; the skinnier, the better.

Unlike the pale skin ideal of the past, white women in the United States today want a sun-kissed face in the United States. The trend is catching on in Asian countries, too. Many women think having a tan makes them look healthy and rich, like Hollywood stars. Drugstores sell bronzed skin in a bottle, and both men and women flock to tanning salons to lie under a lamp or get sprayed with a chemical. Tanned skin has become a status symbol. It is associated with leisure time outdoors today, unlike in the past when it was associated with the lower class working in the fields. If you have time to play sports or lay out on the beach in this business world, you must have money to maintain your year-round tan.

What is rare in the culture often becomes the gold standard for beauty. In Brazil, women want bigger chests, in Japan and Korea, double eyelids and a narrow nose. In the United States, American women want to be thin and young forever, and the most common cosmetic surgeries are liposuction and Botox.

Being thin is a status symbol and is associated with economic success in many countries. In the United States, there is a saying, "You can never be too thin or too rich."

Beauty contests also set unrealistic beauty standards for most women. The average American woman is 5 feet and 4 inches tall (1.64 meters) and weighs 140 lbs. (63.5 kilos). The average Miss America contestant is 5 feet and 8 inches tall (1.73 meters) and weighs 120 lbs. (54 kilos). Only 10% of American women fit the height and weight profile of a professional model. Seven million young women suffer from eating disorders in the United States, and the number is increasing, according to the National Association of Anorexia Nervosa and Associated Eating Disorders (ANAD).

Our eating and exercise habits have not kept pace with the beauty standards in our heads. Most women read fashion magazines or watch the Miss America pageant and feel bad about themselves. We can't compare to the air-brushed or televised models. Through camera and makeup tricks, pounds have melted off the model, makeup has erased her lines on her forehead, and for that matter, any freckles and pimples too.

Just when we become dissatisfied with ourselves, women's magazines advertise "self-esteem." You mean we can look like our models and movie stars displayed on their covers? How do we manage this? Buy these cosmetics, go on this diet, take this vitamin, and we will make ourselves over like Cinderella going to the ball.

Too many bad hair days? A first-rate haircut at this expensive salon, or a $20-dollar gel will make us look like Jennifer Aniston. The cosmetic and hair-care industry convinces American women to constantly change their appearance by spending more money to be beautiful.

Some American women wear quite a bit of makeup, especially eye-shadows, compared to other countries. We put unnatural blues, glittery pinks and other colors on our eyelids that many women from other countries find strange. American women also wear bright red, purple and even glitter nail polish. False fingernails or acrylics are quite common among women. Others paint their nails one color and then put tattoos or designs on top of the nail polish.

A few American magazines have broken with the traditional view of beauty. Instead of putting only thin women on their covers they have included overweight models. Clothing lines for plus-size women are growing in the fashion industry. As sixty percent of Americans are overweight, magazines featuring full-figure models more accurately portray American women today.

Most American women consider men such as Tom Cruise and Denzel Washington classically handsome. Both

actors have highly defined jaws and with no beard or
mustache. They look like the eternal college student, or
what Americans call clean-cut or preppy.

The average American male is 5' 10" inches (1.78
meters) tall and weighs 180 lbs. (82 kilos). Many American
women like tall and muscular men. Men sweat in gyms so
that their biceps pop out like two tennis balls. They believe
the meatier they are, the more handsome they will be.

Fashion

Fashion in the United States is often a matter of
wearing jeans, a T-shirt and tennis shoes most of the time.
Sweat suits made for jogging are now worn to shopping
malls, school and just about everywhere except work.

We Americans compare ourselves to French culture
all the time, yet the rest of the world knows us for our
"low-brow" culture of costume jewelry and sports clothes.
We wear white socks with our tennis shoes everywhere.
In many European countries, white socks are strictly used
for sports or in farming regions. You would be seen as on
your way to the tennis court, for example, and not to the
movies.

Michael Jordan and Madonna did more for the fashion
industry in the United States than many of our fashion
models put together. Jordan started the baggy pants craze
in the 1980's when he wore his basketball uniform under
his regular pants with a big belt and a fad was born.

Madonna changed fashion forever when she brought
bras out of the underwear drawer and wore them publicly.
Today, we have many shirts that are camisoles which in
pre-Madonna days, would have been considered lingerie
for the bedroom.

American casual clothes can shock you with the
intensity and choice of colors. T-shirts, in particular, have
developed into an art form in the United States. They come
in bright orange, hot pink, and loud green. You can find

them with bold stripes, advertising decals and political slogans.

Business attire is more casual here than in Europe and Asia, but it varies with the region. On the East Coast, the suit coat and tie are still worn, and East Coast women wear more neutral colors. Black is seen in New York City more than other parts of the country. In the South, you see more floral designs, dresses and hats. In the West, business attire can be khakis and a polo shirt for men, and suits can be even worn with cowboy boots in the ranching states.

On the West Coast in particular, men in insurance and real estate often wear a nicely pressed shirt and wool pants, but they leave the tie home or the suit coat in the office when they go to lunch. If you look too fashionable in California, people think you look overdressed. Many employees love Fridays as it is often a "dress down" day. This is when you can even wear jeans to work.

Doggies, Kitties & Birdies

Chapter 14:

Pets as Partners

S ixty-three percent of American households own a pet, according to a 2007/2008 survey by the American Pet Products Manufacturers Association. We are truly a pet loving nation. Many Americans view pets as a member of the family, even as partners. More than half of American dog owners are more attached to their pets than to another human being, reports the American Pet Association in 2003. Most American dogs sleep in the bed with their owners and 67% of America's cats do. And some 39% of America's pet owners display their pet's picture in their home.

Americans love a variety of pets, but most of all, we love our dogs. We kiss dogs on the mouth, give them manicures and throw them birthday parties. We have doggie beaches and bakeries. We have plastic bags provided by beaches and parks to clean up dog waste.

American customs and attitudes toward their dogs and cats are based on our own personal needs. The explosion

Out of the Doghouse...

and into the Beauty Parlor...

Pet Signature Clothing – Dress your pet in style.

Pet Massages – To rejuvenate muscles and joints.

Pet Sitters – Drop off your pet at a daycare center or at a friend's house.

Pet Videos – When you are away at work, your pet no longer has to feel lonely.

Pet Beauty Line – *Fauna*, a Santa-Monica based company offers all-natural bath line for pets. Stamped with people tested, pet-approved.

Pet Health Insurance – To insure against the high cost of illness and accidents.

Pet Nail Polish – OPI, a leading nail polish brand for women, has now designed nail polish specifically for pets' nails. It is called Pet Pawlish. Now pet owners can give their pets a beautiful pet-i-cure.

of pets seems to show how lonely we are as a nation for companionship. Families are getting smaller and a growing number of singles, childless couples and older people look to a pet to keep them company.

Historically, the Christian religion has believed in the dominion of humans over animals. Today, however, animals have been raised a notch on the human scale as a growing number of Americans treat them as children. When we talk to them, we often say "Good boy!" and "Good girl!" instead of "Good dog! or "Good cat!"

Laws are being adapted to the changing ways of thinking about pets in the United States. Pet trusts are becoming popular in a growing number of states. Currently, nineteen of the fifty states allow pet owners to set up a trust fund for the care, feeding and medical treatment of their pets if the owners die.

New laws have been passed in several U.S. cities and one state (Rhode Island) to change the term pet "owner" to "guardian" to refer to the relationship between owners and their pets. The idea is that by changing the term to "guardians," people will treat their pets more humanely if they see themselves as caregivers and protectors rather than property owners. Similarly, when animal shelters place pets in new homes, they call this process "adopting a pet."

Americans spend $150 million a year on pet pain medicines alone and more and more pet owners are investing in pet health insurance. We are prolonging pet lifespans with medicines that have been traditionally reserved for humans. Pets in the United States get radiation therapy, hip replacements, organ transplants and high-tech diagnostic procedures such as magnetic resonance imaging. Specialized veterinary medicine is a booming industry.

There is even a new airline exclusively for pets, PetAirways, which has recently begun operating in the U.S.

Owners drop their pet off at a Pet Lounge, and pets ride in a secured crate in the plane's cabin and are monitored every 15 minutes during the flight. This is unlike other airlines, which usually put animals in the cargo hold.

Animal shelters have been set up in the United States for abused pets. You can call a government protection agency for pets. If a neighbor reports signs of pet abuse, the animal control agency will come and may take the pet away to an animal shelter to protect it.

Stray cats and dogs that seem to be without owners are not seen very much on the streets in the United States. If a stray dog or cat is seen roaming the street in the United States, someone in the neighborhood usually calls the local Animal Control agency and an official comes to fetch the animal and take it to an animal shelter too. Since there are too many dogs and pets in the United States, animal shelters are forced to kill hundreds of thousands of dogs and cats each year.

Disney animated movies help very little in controlling our impulse to buy a pet we might not be able to take care of. They show cute animals that talk and sing, which motivates some Americans to go out and buy a pet shown in the movie. Clown fish sold briskly in pet stores when the movie *Finding Nemo* was released.

When the movie *101 Dalmatians* came out some years ago, it caused people to run to the pet store and scoop up a frisky Dalmatian dog. Many of these impulsive owners eventually gave these animals to the animal shelters, as they realized, over time, that they couldn't take care of them.

Becoming a vegetarian is the ultimate statement in favor of animals for some people. Many vegetarians in the United States eat no meat, not for health reasons but for the love of animals.

Animal rights activists in the United States have been very influential in elevating pets to near human status.

These groups target different animals to be saved, organize campaigns and are highly visible as they get out on the streets and protest. They first started out opposing animals being used for fur by throwing paint and blood on the fur coats of fashionable ladies coming out of department stores. Now, very few Americans wear real fur. Another issue was dolphins being trapped in tuna fishermen's nets. Animal rights groups won that battle too. Now tuna cans sold in the United States are labeled *"dolphin-safe."* Animal testing for cosmetics has greatly decreased and now many of our shampoo bottles and cosmetic packages print *"no animal testing."*

The activities of some animal rights groups have even turned violent. Ecological groups and animal-rights extremists have been responsible for an estimated 1,100 violent acts since 1976, the FBI reported in a hearing before Congress. The violent tactics of the animal extremists focus their attacks on medical and research labs at universities.

Attitudes toward dogs vary according to culture. In Muslim countries, they are largely seen as unclean and a source of spreading diseases. In Singapore, Hong Kong and South Korea, dog soup is considered a hearty soup. In Latin America, they are not treated the same as in the United States. Stray dogs roaming in the street are seen as dangerous and aggressive.

In Asian countries, space largely dictates the kind of pet you can have. Fish and birds are more common than dogs and cats, as they take up less space. Large pets are forbidden in most Japanese apartments. Also, Japan is very hygiene conscious, and if the Japanese have a dog, they usually don't sleep with their owners.

However, the trend of owning a pet is a growing phenomenon in other countries too. Traditionally, dogs and cats have been fed the leftovers or food scraps off the dinner table, without buying commercial pet food in the stores. But now, pet food sales are exploding, reports the

Pet Food Institute. The Korean market for pet food alone has increased 600 percent over the past 10 years. Latin America is buying more pet food too, as pet ownership is becoming more popular, and feeding pets commercially prepared food is on the rise.

Notes

"Acquiring a dog may be the only time a person gets to choose a relative."

– Unknown

Got Checks?

To Pay Bills

Many Americans still write personal checks at home and send the checks by mail.

7-Eleven Convenience Stores

While 7-Elevens are known in the U.S. for its huge soft-drinks like Big Gulps and Slurpees, in Thailand and Japan, people pay electric and telephone bills there.

Post Offices

In many European and Asian countries, you can do banking at the post office or in some cases, even pay bills there too.

Got Cash?

ATMs in cash-oriented countries can give out more cash to their bank customers than in the U.S.

In Latin American countries, credit cards are usually limited to high-income individuals because interest rates are quite high.

Chapter 15:

Dreaming of Dollars

W hy is it sometimes hard to rent an apartment without a U.S. credit card? Newcomers are often frustrated to learn that even with a credit card from their country and money in their banks, landlords may be reluctant to rent to people who don't have a "paper trail" or a history of using credit cards in the United States. A person's credit history seldom transfers from one country to another because of privacy laws and different credit reporting standards. Foreign residents often have to pay cash for security deposits before they establish a credit history here.

In contrast, Americans can only take out $300 cash a day from a ATM cash machine yet we can get a credit card limit of thousands of dollars. Once we have one credit card, letters arrive in the mail offering us more credit cards.

Special Treatment and Tipping

In a society where everyone is supposed to be treated equally, Americans secretly want to be treated special, like a king or queen. Ask us about our vacations, and instead of describing the places and people, we'll begin to tell you about all the luxuries of the beautiful hotel with a swimming pool, and the way people treated us like royalty.

We are the biggest tippers in the world because we tip to show how well servers treated us more than how fast they served us. While most countries have a service charge included in the restaurant bill or a much smaller tip such as 10%, we have a 15-20% "voluntary donation." Many international visitors reluctantly tip if the service is good but what happens if the service is bad? A tip of 10% or less usually makes a statement that the service was poor.

The word *tips* is said to have originated from an acronym, "to insure prompt service," dating back to sixteenth-century England. Customers would give the waiter money *before* they were served, and the tip amount would determine how well they were treated.

The quality of the service in restaurants in the United States greatly depends on the individual server who waits on you. You might get servers who take a long time to bring your meal and look overworked. Then there are the overenthusiastic servers whose presentation of the daily specials resembles performance art. They eagerly give us so many options that we cannot remember any particular dish.

Americans usually tip whether or not the service was poor or even when there were too many interruptions by an overeager waiter. We generally feel sorry for the low wages that waiters earn, which is usually close to minimum wage plus tips. Tips have spread to fast-food eateries and self-service cafes. Today, you may see a giant jar for tips next to the cash register, even though no one has given you personal table service.

Money Habits

Americans talk about money freely when it relates to the state of the economy or how much things cost in general. Yet our own money is considered nobody's business, and subject of personal finances is considered a taboo topic.

In many families, only the mother and father discuss money and manage the household finances. They don't inform the children. Young people get their first job as teenagers and begin to manage their money with little guidance. We have learned to spend through an allowance, but we have not been taught to save. The majority of Americans households, 74%, are in debt, and are paying on mortgages, car loans or credit cards. In addition, American families owe an average of 7,300 in credit card debt according to the 2009 Survey of Consumer Finances issued by the U.S. Federal Reserve.

Some Americans try to become rich and famous as quickly as possible. We play the lottery or gamble in casinos, not only in Las Vegas but also on Indian reservations or off-shore ships. On TV, *Joe Millionaire* was a popular show among young people. Women wanted to date this American bachelor who was supposed to be a millionaire. When the women in the contest found out that the bachelor wasn't a millionaire after all, most of them were disillusioned and lost interest in him.

Learning Annex, a school for working adults, offers classes such as, "Smart Couples Finish Rich," "How to Think Like the Rich," "Make $$$ as a Researcher," "Earn a $1,000 a day as a Personal Coach," and "How to Hide Your Assets and Disappear."

Americans love to hear stories of people from humble beginnings who become rich from their hard work and personal initiative. In school, we learn about Abraham Lincoln and other heroes who went from rags to riches. Parents ask children what they want to be when they are growing up. A doctor? A lawyer? They tell their children that they can be anything they want regardless of talent or economic limitations.

Then when young people graduate from high school and take their first full-time job, they become disillusioned. Many earn minimum wage. Weren't they going to be rich and famous just like their parents and schools told them?

When foreigners see an American writing a check in the supermarket, they are amazed. Why are Americans so attached to checks? We still use checks when other countries use cash, pay online, or by credit card. In fact, the United States was the only country that saw growth in check use in today's world of electronic banking.

The average American writes 15 checks a month, according to a recent Federal Reserve report. Sixty percent of our non-cash transactions are with a check. We pay most of our bills with a check and send it through the mail. In many countries in Latin America, the people go in person to the post offices or utility companies to pay their bills.

In Europe, debit and credit cards are more widely used than here. In some Western European countries, people must pay a small fee to write a check. This charge discourages people from writing checks. Americans like the fact that there is a time lapse of about a day before the check is cashed.

Even American retailers like checks, now that they have a little machine to verify that the funds to cover the check are in the customer's bank account. With this machine, the cost of processing a check is cheaper than processing a credit card.

The American dollar is also called a "buck." This nickname for the dollar can be traced to our colonial days, when we used buckskins, or the hides of a male deer, as a money substitute. Compared to the colorful paper money of other countries, our dollar bills are not exactly exciting. The Eurobills, for example, display colorful architecture of member countries.

We have dead presidents and major political figures on

one side of the bills and political buildings on the other. Only once did a woman appear on a U.S. bill. Martha Washington, the wife of our founding president, appeared on $1 silver certificate in the late 1880's. We have failed to represent important women in our history on our bills, while countries such as Germany, Denmark, and Sweden have had many outstanding women depicted on their bills.

The U.S. Treasury Department has redesigned our dollar bills in the past few years to help the blind and visually impaired. The government has added color to the bills, made the portraits of the presidents and political statesmen much larger, and has added security features such as watermarks.

Our dollar bills have been redesigned largely because of a successful lawsuit brought by a Washington D.C. lawyer Jeffrey Lovitky in memory of his legally-blind physician wife. When Lovitky's wife, Sandra Welner, died in 2001, Lovitky wanted to do something that would celebrate his wife's legacy and affect millions of people. Lovitky remembered how he would have to sort his wife's dollar bills and put the different denominations in envelopes before she went on trips.

So in 2002, Lovitky sued the Treasury Department. He represented the American Council of the Blind and argued that the failure to design a currency that is accessible to blind people is a form of discrimination. It took four years in order for a federal appeals court to rule in his favor which resulted in the redesign of the entire U.S. currency.

For coins, the United States once minted a silver dollar with a woman on it. Susan B. Anthony, a leader in the 19th century women's rights movement, was the first woman to appear on a coin. Today, Sacagawea, an Indian woman with her child strapped to her back, appears on a gold dollar coin. She was instrumental to the success of the Lewis and Clark expedition and exploration of the Missouri River. This gold coin can be requested at local banks, and is sometimes available at post offices.

Status or Pay?

There is a major difference between the social status of a job and what it pays in the U.S. as shown below in the two tables.

The Most Prestigious Jobs

1. Firefighter
2. Scientist
3. Teacher
4. Doctor
5. Military Officer
6. Nurse
7. Police Officer
8. Priest/Minister/Clergy
9. Farmer
10. Engineer

Source: The Harris Poll, #77, Aug. 1, 2007

The Best Paid Jobs

1. Anesthesiologist
2. Surgeon
3. Obstetrician/Gynecologist
4. Orthodontist
5. Oral/Maxillofacial Surgeon
6. General Internist
7. Prosthodontists
8. Psychiatrist
9. Family & General Practitioner
10. Chief Executive

Source: Bureau of Labor Statistics, 2007

Chapter 16:

Work: 24/7

W hy do Americans work so hard? Many people think the Protestant work ethic drives Americans to work long hours. This may have been the case in the past, but not anymore. Companies have been downsizing, and threat of getting laid off is very real today. Americans now work longer hours, and often do the work of two or three people because they are afraid of losing their jobs. They work hard to become valuable to the company so that if and when the company lays off employees, the boss will keep them on staff.

How obsessed are Americans with work? This can be measured if you take a day off. If you happen to run into someone on the street while doing errands, they will ask you, "You mean you're not working today?" That may lead to, "Are you still working at the same place?" to confirm you are not laid off.

Your job identifies you more than anything else in the United States, except for race or ethnicity. Americans question each other, and the questions usually follow a certain order, such as, "What's your name?" Then if you look physically different or have a foreign-sounding name, it will be followed by, "Where are you from?" We continue with our identification process until we get to, "What do you do?"

The most powerful excuse you can give someone when they invite you somewhere and you would rather not go is, "I have to work." No more questions will be asked. The other person will understand and think work always comes before a social engagement. Compare this to, "I'm busy." You might get more questions as to when your appointment is and insistence that you come after your social commitment.

In the United States, you can be hired relatively easily, compared to other countries. Many people do not have employment contracts in the United States. When workers are hired for a job, their salary, working hours and benefits are often discussed in the hiring interview. At the end of this interview, the employer and the new employee trust each other with a simple verbal agreement called a "gentlemen's agreement" when it is followed by a handshake. Some employers, however, require you to have a medical exam, a background check, or a second interview before they will actually hire you.

Getting fired or dismissed is fairly easy too. Usually, an employee is given two chances to make major mistakes, through a verbal and a written warning. If the work performance hasn't changed by the third time, an employer can fire them. Policies toward work performance and behavior vary widely, but many workplaces have a "zero tolerance" policy for alcohol and drug use. If employers catch an employee working either while drinking or high on drugs, it is possible that the employee could be fired immediately.

If you are unemployed in the United States, you usually use up your savings, if you have any. You can file for unemployment, but the federal government gives you money for just six months. A check for unemployment is usually less than half of the salary you earned, so it is an impossible amount to survive on.

Many Americans do not have a family network to help them in times of job loss and so we work doubly hard. We tend not to have much savings either, and so we commonly say, "We don't have anything to fall back on."

We work an average of 40 hours a week, census data shows, but this doesn't reflect the reality of work today. With the Internet and cell phone an integral part of the work day, we now have the tools to take our job home. We also bring our laptops to work on the plane, on the beach, in bed, and even on vacation. We have "working lunches," "working dinners," and "working vacations." Our work day has stretched into many unofficial hours, averaging another 10-20 hours a week with our electronic cords.

You often hear that time is money in the United States. Even though you hear Americans complain about never having enough time, money is actually more important than time to us, according to a recent Roper survey. When the survey gave a choice between more money or more time, 56% of Americans chose money, while only 35% wanted more time.

The computer has been quickly replacing jobs in the United States, as it is in other countries. However, in the United States, the manufacturing sector has been moving abroad at a rapid pace to reduce labor costs. American corporations have been able to lay off workers with relative ease without paying employees severance pay or medical insurance.

This differs from other countries where labor laws or government controls are stronger. Labor unions have been decreasing steadily since the 1940's. Only 13% of the American workplace is unionized, mainly in the auto, construction, and mining industries. When we know that a computer can replace us at any time, we are demoralized and our loyalty to a company is affected. We are apt to change jobs more frequently as we see our jobs as disposable.

Praise in the Workplace

American employees are generally used to continuous verbal feedback from their employer. Much of the feedback is positive in the form of praise, "Good job!" "Well done!" and "Keep up the good work!"

In one of my classes with Korean professionals, we did a role-play exercise that revealed a significant cross-cultural difference in dealing with an employee's poor performance. The Koreans were instructed to show what would happen in Korea if an employee missed an important deadline for submitting a financial report. In several of the role-plays, the Korean managers stood very close to their employee's face and loudly scolded the employee while the Korean employee listened and bowed his head in shame.

Then we watched a video of how the U.S. management expert and author Ken Blanchard role-played the same situation. He asked the employee to sit down. Then he said something like, "Though I really value you as an employee, I was disappointed to see that you turned in the report late." Blanchard pointed out the employee's mistake in a factual way without raising his voice and without changing his emotional tone. The Koreans found this American manager's response confusing because he first started out with something positive to say about the employee before he expressed his criticism and so we had a lively discussion afterwards on the cultural differences.

Balancing Work and Family

Sixty percent of American women work, reports the Bureau of Labor Statistics 2008. Many of these women are also mothers. The American workplace, however, has still a long way to go in order to meet the needs of working mothers. It has only been since 1993 that a woman could take three months off for unpaid maternity leave and be guaranteed her job back when she returned.

A federal law called the Family and Medical Leave Act now gives American workers up to 12 weeks a year of unpaid leave to take care of a family member. This policy allows American employees time to have a baby or take care of an elderly parent. The employer, by law, must reserve their positions and seniority in the company until the employees return. This law, however, only applies to companies with 50 or more employees. Since most companies in the United States have fewer than 50 employees, they are not legally obligated to offer this benefit to their workers.

Even when companies offer this benefit, few Americans take advantage of it. There is still the stigma attached to taking personal time off from your job that prevents workers from using this job benefit.

Child care for working parents is also scarce in the United States. There are not many daycare centers or preschools for working parents who have no family members living close by. There are even fewer daycare centers for children under two years old. The cost of insurance is so high for this age group that most daycare/ preschools do not accept very young children. Therefore, many children under two years old are watched by home-based daycare workers. These daycares vary in quality and are often criticized for accepting too many children into one home. You only need minimum training to qualify as a daycare provider before you can set up your home for a babysitting operation. Many housewives earn a good living taking care of infants. The other alternative is for mothers to stay home these first two years. This, however, is not an option for many working families.

Time

Though time may not be as important as earning cash to an American, it is still considered extremely valuable. Future time is valued the most and what happened in the

Personal vs. Professional Life

Americans divide their lives into personal and professional. After working eight or more hours at the job or so-called "professional life," we usually go home to the "personal life" or family.

We usually do not wine or dine with colleagues after work. Bosses usually do not call employees at home unless it's an urgent matter.

I Quit!

Looking for another job is fairly common in the United States. Many Americans plan to change jobs every year, and most of us will have several employers in our lifetime. Americans stay on their jobs for an average of four years, according to the Bureau of Labor Statistics 2008.

Time or Money?

past is valued the least. You can see how the past is often dismissed. "That's history," you hear Americans say, "forget it. Today is different." Future time is valued because we think we can control it. Americans get irritated waiting in grocery lines and when they get caught in traffic because the waiting time is unpredictable and therefore, outside of our control.

When an unexpected tragedy occurs, whether it be wildfires or plane crashes, what is the official American response that you see published in the newspapers? It is not an emotional reaction but a measured one, "We are determining the cause of the accident. An investigation as to the cause has been ordered." We think we can still do something even when there is nothing to do.

The notion of a country living on future time is evident in the buying of insurance. We must buy car insurance by law, "in case we have an accident." Buying insurance of any sort calms us down and erases the worries of future accidents.

We have mortgage insurance "in case we lose our jobs." We have health insurance, "in case we get sick." We have life insurance, "in case we die and no one has money to hold a funeral and bury us properly." Some people even buy flight insurance "in case the plane goes down."

We have fire drills in schools and workplaces, "in case of a fire," and, in some parts of the country, "in case of an earthquake." This "in case of an accident" mentality is shortened in our minds and we often simply say, "just in case." The bad thing that could possibly happen is implied. We sometimes justify buying many items in the supermarket or stores, stocking up, "just in case." The fear is that the store will stop carrying the item and you will return and be left without a choice.

Some Americans plan their vacations a year in advance and may buy airline tickets up to a month in advance. International visitors and students are bothered when they want to make plans for a weekend in Las Vegas or San

Francisco. After making some phone calls, they realize that the cheapest tickets must be purchased 14 days in advance. Two weeks? They want to go in two days. In some countries, the best rates can be had with one-week notice, and in other countries there is no discount for advance reservations, so planning in advance is not rewarded.

Wasting time is highly subjective. If you take a vacation and it's not heavily programmed into a schedule of activities, or you are not going out of town, Americans might consider it a waste of time.

Americans have agendas in their hands and calendars on their minds. Time is a product to the American psyche. We buy and spend it, borrow and lend it. There is a good time and a bad time to do something. "One thing at a time," we say when we want to slow things down. We find and lose time, set or schedule time. Something takes up time, and we make up time. We are behind or ahead of time according to the hands of a clock. We reward people for being on time. Most movie theaters and restaurants seat you on a first come, first served basis. Though many Americans tend to be punctual for work, we are much less so for personal engagements. Again, we want to control our time and choose our time of arrival over someone else's. For a social occasion, Americans will usually tolerate latecomers for a ten to fifteen-minute grace period before they leave, make new plans, or cancel reservations.

Measuring on an American Ruler

You walk into a McDonald's in France and there is no such thing as a "Quarter Pounder with Cheese." Instead, they offer a "Hamburger Royale with Cheese." The measurement of a quarter of a pound is not understood by most of the world, and it is like speaking a foreign tongue.

The United States is one of the few countries that clings to the English Imperial system. Why doesn't the United

States have the metric system when the rest of world does?

That is a question we have been trying to answer since we started to convert to the metric system in 1975, without much success. We first tried to convert the road signs to have both English miles and metric kilometers. What happened? We went back to the miles again. We never really changed. We just experimented with converting to the metric system.

It has been a constant battle, as our system is so tied to the beginning of our country. American colonists adopted the English or Imperial system of inches, pounds, and miles when our country first developed. The British system dates back to the reign of King Henry I (1100-1135) when the royal government made the 12-inch foot official.

The metric system, on the other hand, is much younger. It dates back only to the French Revolution of 1789. Great Britain, at that time was very anti-French and didn't want anything to do with French changes, and so the Imperial system continued in England and the United States, while the rest of the world adopted the much easier French measurement system where things can be divided by ten.

The U.S. federal government has been trying to lead the public by labeling food products with both the metric and the English system. The U.S. military has basically changed to the metric system too.

In the global economy, many Americans cannot measure properly today because they are taught two systems of measurement in our schools. Our system is much harder to learn. With three feet to a yard and 12 inches to a foot, the base number of 10 in the metric system is easier. We are taught metric too, but very briefly, and the end result of this two-tracked system is that many students can't measure accurately in either system.

Some scholars believe that our clinging to the English measurement system has hurt American students when they compete against international students in math and science tests. On the Third International Math and Science Test, American students had to do all the math work in metric. This worked to their disadvantage, as many are not proficient in that measurement system. If they had grown up with the metric system, they might have done better on the math portion and would have been more competitive with their international counterparts.

If the United States goes metric, it will shake up not only the educational system, but will also radically change the way we do many things here. It's in our English vocabulary. In traffic, "We haven't moved an inch." (At all.) In complaining, "If you give an inch, they take a mile." (If you give a little to someone, they will take a lot.)

All our football fields would have to be lengthened in our stadiums, going to 100 meters instead of 100 yards. Even when the National Football League started a European League, the fields were measured in yards.

Though the sport of track has already changed to metric, people still refer to the 880 or the 220, which are English units, not metric. Although the races are in metric distances, the field events, such as the high jump, long jump, and pole vault, still use the English system.

Construction contractors would have to change the way they measure to build houses and commercial buildings. It would require every tool and piece of equipment made in the United States to be torn apart and refigured in metric parts.

Going metric would take a huge investment of money in the short term, but in the long term it would save Americans money. It would eliminate the costly two-system approach and help us master one measurement system rather than being mediocre in both. As far as competing in a global economy, it would make trade easier with our international counterparts and deepen our understanding of our global partners.

Notes

"The best way to appreciate your job is to imagine yourself without one."

– Oscar Wilde, humorist (1856-1900)

I Pledge Allegiance

I pledge allegiance
To the flag
Of the United States of America,
And to the Republic
For which it stands,
One nation,
Under God,
Indivisible,
With liberty and justice for all.

Chapter 17:

Flag Fever

W hy are Americans so patriotic? The American flag waves to us from front porches, car antennas, and hotel rooftops. We wear flag pins on our coats and t-shirts. Signs in people's windows read, "Proud to be an American."

Most Americans do love their country and are proud of it, polls report.

Although Americans take pride in their individuality, when we show our patriotism, we act with a group mentality like never before. Many people display the U.S. flag outside their homes for patriotic holidays.

Our patriotism is often judged by flying or swearing to our flag. We stand up and sing the national anthem before sporting events. Students must face the flag and swear to be loyal to their country from elementary through high school with the Pledge of Allegiance. Immigrants who become naturalized citizens swear to be loyal to the United States and give up all their loyalty to their country of origin.

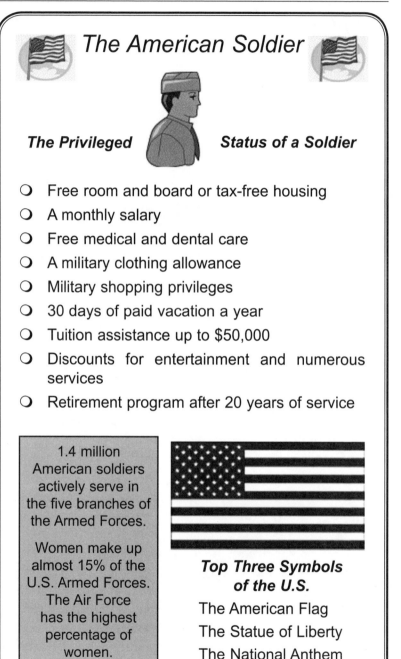

The American Soldier

The Privileged   Status of a Soldier

- Free room and board or tax-free housing
- A monthly salary
- Free medical and dental care
- A military clothing allowance
- Military shopping privileges
- 30 days of paid vacation a year
- Tuition assistance up to $50,000
- Discounts for entertainment and numerous services
- Retirement program after 20 years of service

1.4 million American soldiers actively serve in the five branches of the Armed Forces.

Women make up almost 15% of the U.S. Armed Forces. The Air Force has the highest percentage of women.

Top Three Symbols of the U.S.
The American Flag
The Statue of Liberty
The National Anthem

Source: U.S. Department of Defense

The flag is a powerful symbol in this country. In the U.S., we have few majestic cathedrals, archeological ruins and palaces to point to with an historic sense of pride as many other countries do. We also lack royal figures such as the Queen of England or the King of Thailand who are potent symbols that often unite a nation's people. We have so many people from various cultures living together in the U.S. that we might feel more "united" as a people by flying our national flag. This may be one of the reasons why Americans give more emotional weight to the flag than a mere representation of our country.

How patriotic are Americans? If patriotism means love of one's country, then Americans appear to be strongly patriotic. In a 33-country survey done by the University of Chicago in 2006, national pride was measured in ten specific areas of society. Americans said that they were the most proud of their country in five of the ten areas: their democracy, political influence, economic system, science and their military. In order to measure general national pride, the survey asked people of their respective countries to agree with such statements as "I would rather be a citizen of my country than any other country in the world," and "Generally speaking, my country is a better country than most countries." Of the 33 countries assessed, the U.S. ranked second in national pride, second only to Venezuela.

We also show our patriotism through military service. We have one million, four hundred thousand soldiers in the United States. The U.S. by far leads the world in military spending, according to the Center for Defense Information. The U.S. military budget for the fiscal year 2008 was 711 billion dollars. The 2008 military budget included supplemental funds for the wars in Iraq and Afghanistan.

To put these numbers in context, the Center for Arms Control and Non-Proliferation reports in 2008 that U.S. military spending represents 48% or nearly half of the world's military spending. The U.S. military budget is eight times larger than China's, whose military budget is at 81 billion and is the second largest military spender in the world.

Roughly one million of our 1.4 million American troops are stationed in the United States. The rest are serving abroad. Most of our military personnel have been permanently stationed in Germany, Japan, and South Korea. Our military commitments overseas are in the process of change, however, with massive deployments in Afghanistan and Iraq.

The "new normal" for Americans is reading daily news reports of military casualties in Afghanistan and Iraq. According to the Defense Department's report and as of press time, 4,300 U.S. military troops have been killed in the Iraq war since March 2003. At least 683 U.S. military troops have also died in Afghanistan since 2001.

The political and social impact of our military troops stationed around the world affects the way people from other cultures view Americans. To be fair, overseas military bases exist to defend against potential military threats. The social problems caused in the host country may be interpreted as a price to pay for that protection. But we cannot deny that our military presence is often a source of anger for many local citizens living near military bases in Japan, South Korea, Germany and Italy.

In a re-organization of our U.S. military, some of our U.S. marines stationed in Okinawa, Japan have recently relocated to the U.S. territory of Guam. Military troops based in central Seoul, South Korea also plan to move 45 miles (65 kilometers) south of Seoul, into Pyeongtaek as our military troops presence there has been a constant source of anti-American protests.

The American military has been an entirely voluntary service since 1973. Many young high school graduates sign up or enlist for two to four years, depending on the branch of service, mainly because of the benefits that the federal government promises.

After completing your service, military benefits include the federal government paying for your college. The U.S. government also helps with a mortgage if veterans want to buy a house, and provides special medical insurance along with many more lifetime benefits.

In our presidential elections, we have a relatively low voter turnout. We do not have to vote by law, it is entirely voluntary. Fewer than half of eligible Americans vote for the president. The people who do vote usually fall into two parties, the Democrats and the Republicans, with a very small percentage divided into smaller, independent parties. If you divide the 50% of the voting public into two parties of 25% each and then reduce that number to account for those who vote for smaller, independent parties, you will have the true number of people electing the president. In other words, around 20% of the people elect the president of the United States. The 2009 election of President Barack Obama, however, was historic as a total of 58.6% percent of the voting public cast a ballot in that election.

Finally, there have been times in history where U.S. presidents have been elected without the majority of the popular vote. If the presidential candidate wins a majority of electoral votes, the state's entire block of votes usually goes to the party candidate. Critics of this "winner take all" electoral system point to the possibility of electing a President who loses the popular vote. This has happened in our political history with John Quincy Adams in 1824, Rutherford B. Hayes in 1876, Benjamin Harrison in 1888, and most recently, with George W. Bush in 2000.

Shop Till You Drop!

All Roads Lead to the Shopping Mall
Buses usually run express services to the shopping malls across the United States.

Mall-rats
Teens often use the shopping malls as social gathering places. They set trends in fashion that younger children often want to follow.

Children Spend at an Early Age
Through advertising and TV exposure, young American children learn brand names when they are in elementary school. The number of children who are spending on their own is increasing. American children also have a big influence on what kinds of food their parents buy when they do their weekly grocery shopping.

Living with Less
With consumer debt and personal bankruptcies on the rise, a movement to simplify our lives is spreading across the United States as evidenced by recent book titles:

- *Choosing Simplicity* by Linda Breen Pierce
- *The Simple Living Guide* by Janet Luhrs

Chapter 18:

Material Girls & Boys

We are one of the most materialistic nations on the planet. Americans collect more things than most people in other countries can imagine, and we spend an enormous amount of time maintaining them.

Some of our garages are so crammed with junk that the car has to be parked in the driveway or the street.

Many museums in the United States are not showcases of paintings or sculpture; they house collections of ordinary objects instead. There are surfboard museums, guitar museums, and computer museums. You name the object, most likely there is a museum for that object somewhere in the United States.

You can really see our materialism at American birthday parties. They have become a huge business. Parents give their 5 year-olds a party full of expensive entertainment. They rent a site at a restaurant such as *Chuck E. Cheese* and give their children complete freedom. The birthday child and the guests play the machines or games after blowing out the candles on the birthday cake. If parents have the birthday party at home, they often rent a trampoline, an Astro Jump, or hire clowns to paint faces or give pony rides.

Actually, children no longer have to wait for their birthday or Christmas to receive gifts. Parents shower them with toys all year long. An American child's bedroom is filled with not one or two stuffed animals but dozens of them. The number of toys a typical child owns is shocking to people of other countries. Yet a common complaint from American children is that they are bored. How is that possible?

Parents usually plan an elaborate birthday celebration when their children turn 16, especially for girls. Sweet sixteen is seen as a passage to womanhood and many families throw a huge party for their daughters. Some parents even rent a room in a hotel or hall so their daughter and friends can dance until the early morning hours.

Then there is prom night, which is a formal dance in high school. Girls and boys usually wear formal gowns and tuxedos and rent a limo to go the school dance. By the time graduation rolls around, the parties have gotten bigger and the spending more lavish.

This is how the simplest of activities, having a birthday or being with friends, has been commercialized and centered on buying things to display rather than on being with people.

Americans generally believe technology solves problems, not people, or that money can buy most solutions. If their child has a problem, parents buy tutoring sessions. If Americans go camping once a year, they might buy enough equipment to live in the forest for two months.

Is there a counterculture in the United States that offers us an alternative to the materialism? Yes, but it is very small. People who actively try to change their lifestyle to a less materialistic one are usually concerned about the protection of the environment or going back to the simple life.

Shopping

We really don't need human contact, or even have to speak English well, to shop in the United States. Of course, we can buy on-line, as some Americans do. But, more frequently, we go into a shop to touch and handle the merchandise and, in the case of clothes, to try them on. Price tags are openly displayed on the merchandise. In some countries, items are often hidden behind the counter and we must ask the store clerk to see them. In the United States, the price is the same for everyone, even if you have a foreign accent.

We are able to pick up and handle items to inspect them in stores without any obligation to buy them. We can try on clothes for an hour and then walk away with a "No, thanks." Salesclerks demonstrate how electronic items work and provide a lot of information before we decide to buy an item.

In other countries, the pricing of items is very different from ours. The price of something has a range and the customer must bargain for the best price he can get from the seller. In some countries, as soon as the salesclerk finds out you are from out of town or a foreigner, the price may be higher because they assume all foreigners are rich. Or in a department store, the clerk may have some leeway as to what price to charge the customer.

In any case, the negotiation of a price and the need to ask for merchandise behind the counter all demand more human contact and language skills than here.

If we don't see a price tag in the United States, many stores now offer electronic scanners to the consumer in the store. We no longer have to hunt down a salesclerk or wait until we get to the cash register.

A unique feature in American stores is our ability to

return merchandise after we have purchased it. Customer service counters are found in most stores, where we can get a refund, store credit, or an exchange. A refund is given when you return the item you bought, with the receipt, and you want to receive cash back. A store credit is when you don't have the receipt for the item you purchased; the store then gives credit equal to the amount of the item's purchase. An exchange is used when the item purchased is damaged or not working in some way and the customer wants the same thing, but in good condition. You leave the defective item at the customer service counter and look for another similar item in the store without any exchange of money.

Shopping is addictive in the United States. Few of us need an excuse to shop today. There are people who need to shop every day to feel good, true shopaholics. Of course, few foreign visitors escape the seductive power of stores in advertising their wares, and use much of their spare time shopping, too.

Nearly all of our holidays in the United States have lost their original meaning and have turned into shopping holidays. Substantial sales are also tied to a particular day to get us in the door and spending our money.

Of course, if we wait for a sale to be tied to a season, there are only four seasons, and four sales are not nearly enough. This is why we have a President's Day sale, a Memorial Day sale, a Labor Day sale, a Columbus Day sale, a Veterans Day sale, a Thanksgiving sale, and sales before and after Christmas.

In such a competitive business, stores do not merely announce they have reduced prices or discounts. No, it's a war out there. We use violent images of a sword or at least a knife. Prices have been cut. Sales are described as *slashing prices, price cuts* or *blow-outs*. Many Americans buy the daily newspaper just for the ads. Buying a local newspaper in the United States would virtually disappear if it were not for the store ads and customer coupons.

Notes

"Junk is something you keep for years and then throw out two weeks before you need it."

– Source Unknown

The Stagecoach

The stagecoach era only lasted twenty years, 1849-1869, before the railroad put an end to this method of transportation. However brief in our history, the stagecoach has become part of the mythology of our country. It has become a symbol of limitless mobility, adventure and escape. Today, the car and the road trip still express the freedom to move wherever we want.

In Search of the American Cowboy

In American Westerns, we idealize the cowboy, symbolized in John Wayne. Few people know that cowboys usually were very young boys, 12-17 year-olds. Most cowboys retired by the age of 40, making John Wayne more of a romanticized icon than an actor playing an historical role.

American Westerns

Western TV programs such as *Bonanza* and the *Little House on the Prairie*, captured the historical era of the American Frontier.

Chapter 19:

Coast to Coast

I t takes anywhere from three to seven days to drive across the United States, a country that is 2,800 miles wide (4,514 kilometers) and 1,200 miles (2,023 kilometers) long.

Many people dream of packing up their belongings in the car and making a cross-country road trip. A five-hour plane ride definitely sounds more comfortable, but not nearly as romantic, as a road trip from one coast to the other. If you were traveling from the East Coast to the West in the past, the journey was not even close to being romantic.

The stagecoach and wagon 150 years ago brought Midwesterners and some Easterners across the prairies from St. Louis to San Francisco on a journey that usually lasted from 4-5 months because of the poor conditions of the roads.

If you came from the East Coast, you were likely to take a three-month boat ride, which would take you to

Coast to Coast

How can we tell if someone is from Los Angeles or New York?

Los Angeles   **New York**

Los Angelenos...	**New Yorkers...**
Go to nail salons	Go to delis
Drink smoothies	Drink black coffee
Carry water bottles	Carry newspapers
Wear sunglasses	Wear raincoats
Wear pastel colors or Hawaiian shirts	Wear a lot of black & closed-toe shoes
Are laid back and mellow	Are hyper & uptight
Use "dude" & first names	Use last names more

Panama. There, you would get off the ship, walk the 10-mile (16 kilometers) strip of land, or go by pack mule to the other side to get to the Pacific Ocean, board another ship when it came, and head north to the first port of call in the United States, San Diego.

Going through Panama was a shortcut. The long way, which many people took, was to take a ship all around the tip of South America, a voyage that could take at least six months.

Today, you can even walk all the way across the country following a national trail that will take you about 18 months. The American Discovery Trail is the "Route 66" for American hikers or bikers. Established in 2000, it is a coast-to-coast trail that stretches across 15 states, and goes through cities, mountains and deserts, and is for serious bikers or hearty back-packers with time on their hands.

Regional Differences

A popular saying reflects the regional differences in the United States. In Boston, people ask what kind of family you come from; in New York, they ask how much money you make, and in Los Angeles, they ask what kind of car you drive.

What people value distinguishes a region, but through radio, television, and now the Internet, our collective consciousness in the United States has grown. Still, local peculiarities identify the major regions.

In the Southeastern part of the United States, the Southern dialect is the most distinguishing factor. People in the southeast of the country speak with a rising and falling intonation, in a drawn-out way known as the Southern Drawl. It sounds something like this, *"Y'all want a cup of tea?"*

The pace of life is also slower in the South. Though the Civil War ended in 1865, some Southerners still harbor ill feelings toward Yankees, since the Northerners won the war. A Confederate flag flew on the county courthouse in South Carolina until only recently, when the Supreme Court forced the flag to be taken down.

The Northeast is full of Yankees. This is what Americans call people living in the northeastern region of the United States, and it is not a term referring to all Americans, as we are sometimes labeled abroad. New Englanders speak quickly, and also have a strong accent. They tend to drop the "r" after vowels, which is a trademark of a Boston accent. They also draw out the "aw" sound so their coffee sounds like *cawfee*.

Americans divide themselves in half at the Mississippi River. This is how we measure what region we are from. Anything west of the Mississippi is considered the West to most Americans. However, there are variations on this theme. If I talk to Californians and tell them I was born in Michigan, they say, "Oh, you're from the East Coast." If I talk to New Yorkers, it's, "Oh, you're from the Midwest. "

Midwesterners, or those people born in Chicago and Detroit and other industrial cities and towns in this region, are mostly immune to many new trends and foreign influences. This is Middle America, where people are more content with where they live than the rest of the population. It is a region of "steady Eddies." Characterized by other regions as being old-fashioned, they move less than Californians but a bit more than New Englanders.

We can move west until we hit Texas. Texas is a state unto itself. It is the only state that declared itself an independent country for ten years. From 1836-1846, it was the Republic of Texas. Texans have been proud of that fact and call themselves the Lone Star state. The Texas state flag carries one star to represent this unique historical independence.

Texas is portrayed in the media as the land of cowboys and gunslingers. This stereotype is reinforced by western-type clothing. Many Texan men wear a big belt buckle and pointy boots to blend into their Texan landscape. The state of Texas is also noted for its tough enforcement of the death penalty. It doesn't just talk about the death penalty, as many states do, but actually practices it. Texas is the state that actually kills the most death row inmates.

Since 1976, Texas has executed 435 people. This is far ahead of the next execution state, Virginia, which has killed 103 people over that same time period. There is a saying, "Don't mess with Texas." If Texas makes you nervous, you can always move west to California. California is the start-over state.

This notion of moving west and making a fresh start has to do with how California was founded. Gold was discovered in 1848, and California became a state just two years later, completely skipping the intermediate step of being a territory first, because Congress was eager to admit a state with riches.

There was a massive migration of people, called the 49ers, from the East. Most of the 49ers were single men seeking fortunes. While this idea of improving one's lot in life in California stems from the Gold Rush, it is how California is still known today. It's a state that works magic. It's the golden state; it has the Golden Gate.

In California, Los Angeles is the capital of Botox treatments. Keeping a body beautiful is an obsession here. Where else would you find an exercise club on the beach like the one at Venice Beach? There are more nail salons per capita than Boston and its bookstores. The language here is full of *dudes* and *whatevers*, and slang borrowed from surfers.

Since California is such an expensive state to live in today, many people who move to another state are passing it up and heading toward neighboring states. Nevada and Arizona are attracting both immigrants and Americans seeking jobs and lower housing prices.

Among metropolitan cities in the United States, New York City is in a class by itself. Other parts of the country call it neurotic, but it is the only real city in the United

States that feels cosmopolitan when compared to European and Asian cities. What we call urban in the United States seems suburban to many foreigners. The rest of American cities qualify as major metropolitan areas by population only. They retain a small-town feel and the access to public services and commerce is minimal compared to New York.

What about nightlife? Nightlife in the United States is also limited to a few major cities. In many American cities, stores close down after dark and the streets are empty because we are afraid of what might happen to us after 10 p.m. Many of us are also ready for bed around that time anyway in order to get up early for work.

In Brazil, Europe, and other parts of the world, nightlife is just beginning at 10 p.m. In Latin American countries in particular, dancing plays a major role in the country's nightlife. You don't need to go to a club to dance, either, as inviting people to your house and dancing the night away is a common practice on weekends. In Taiwan, there are many teahouses and Internet cafes that offer places for young people to gather at night. In the United States, young people tend to go to bars or dance clubs where you will find mainly other young people.

Notes

"In the United States there is more space where nobody is than where anybody is. That is what makes America what it is."

– Gertrude Stein, American writer (1874-1946)

Romance in the U.S.

Kissing and hugging in public are passionate behaviors commonly called "making out" or public displays of affection. These range from simply hand-holding to grabbing body parts in public.

Americans reactions vary when they see other couples getting physical. Some smile, feel embarrassed or blush and others feel uncomfortable and complain that "it's not polite" or even "it's disgusting." In movies, Americans might call a romantic movie "mushy."

Nicknames for Sweethearts

Americans often use desserts for nicknames when they refer affectionately to each other: Honey, Honeybun, Sweetie, Sweetie pie, Sugar, Sugar pie, Pumpkin. Others: Dear, Darling, Baby, Babe, Precious, Angel, Love and my Better Half.

Classic Pick-Up Lines

- ○ Haven't I seen you before?
- ○ Do you come here often?
- ○ Do you live around here?
- ○ Can I buy you a drink?

Chapter 20:

Mating Rituals

S ex is everywhere in the United States, and available
to all. Meanwhile, arranged marriages continue in
some parts of the world, and women can be stoned
for adultery in other parts of the world.

In the United States, looking for a partner in a country
of self-absorbed and insular people is more difficult than
ever. You can't marry the boy next door because you
barely know your neighbors anymore.

If we didn't widely practice birth control in this country,
we would marry a lot earlier than we do. As it is, 26 and 28
years old is the average age for American women and men
to tie the knot today. We tend to underestimate the power
of birth control and how it affects sexual matters and
dating relationships. It is no coincidence that the founder
of birth control, Margaret Sanger, was one of 11 siblings.

American movies show couples who meet in one
scene and jump into bed in the next. It usually doesn't

Kissing Customs

France – The kissing capital of the world. Start with your left cheek first, normally two kisses are enough, but in Brittany, three is the norm.

Italy – Kissing is for very close friends or family in Italy.

Spain, Austria and Scandinavia – Two kisses. For Spain, you begin the kissing on the right cheek.

Kissing On The Hand – This is considered a great sign of respect and sometimes, adoration.

Kissing On The Head – Shows tender care. Parents sometimes kiss children on their head as a part of a parental blessing.

Blowing A Kiss In The Air – When we are far away from someone, we send them a kiss by air-mail.

Sealed with a Kiss

Where did signing a letter with three XXX's for kisses and three OOO's for hugs come from?

This tradition, also called SWAK, comes from medieval Europe, at a time when many people could not read and write. An important document was usually signed with an X, which was then kissed as a sign of sincerity.

Latin Lovers

In Latin, there are three different words for a kiss, depending on the level of intimacy:

○ An acquaintance kiss – *basium*
○ A close friend's or relative's kiss – *osculum*
○ A lover's kiss – *suavium*

happen that fast. Movies, designed to tell a life story in two hours, omit the development of a relationship and fast-forward to the bed as a way to establish an intimate, physical relationship on the screen.

American men and women tend to be sexually active yes, but not after one date and not with just anybody. Unlike the one-night stands you see in the movies, American women usually go through a series of stages, feelings and commitment before they jump into bed with a boyfriend. In the 1980's, the fear of getting AIDS changed the dating scene in the United States. Carefree sex could now have deadly consequences, and the condom came back to life as a method of prevention of sexually-transmitted diseases.

We are re-discovering our virginity in the United States from campaigns in public schools whose slogan is "Just Say No," to born-again Christians who have decided to become born-again virgins.

After many years of high rates of teenage pregnancy in the United States, the number of pregnancies has leveled off in recent years. Some of this is due to the scare of AIDS, and part of it may be because of the pregnancy prevention taught in schools.

Sexual education is taught in public schools as early as elementary school. Basic short videos begin teaching sex in a scientific way. As students go through junior high, the nature of what they learn becomes less scientific and more practical. By the time Americans reach high school, many are sexually active. They learn about sexually-transmitted diseases, including AIDS, and the focus turns to pregnancy prevention.

Schools have targeted not just women but also men for pregnancy prevention. One such program, called *Baby Think It Over*, requires both male and female high schoolers to take a 7-pound (3.2 kilos) baby doll home over the weekend and care for it 24-hours a day. The electronic doll has been programmed by the teacher to be especially fussy at certain times, so the baby cries when it is hungry or has

Matters of the Heart

When you care about other people or are very giving to others, we say you have **a heart of gold or have a big heart.**

On the other hand, if you are mean and lack compassion, you are **heartless** or **cold-hearted**. When you thank someone and you want to emphasize your appreciation, you can thank him or her **from the bottom of your heart**.

Will You Marry Me?

The average American engagement lasts 16 months, according to the Condé Nast Bridal Group.

○ The average amount spent on a traditional American wedding - $22,000.

○ Popular honeymoon destinations for American newlyweds: Las Vegas, Hawaii, U.S. Virgin Islands, Jamaica and the Bahamas.

○ In Taiwan, the groom's family must pay for all of the wedding expenses. This means the groom's family also decides on the details for the wedding.

a wet diaper. This program has been successful in teaching teenagers in middle and high schools that having a baby is a constant responsibility.

Many American young adults are skeptical and cynical about marriage, since many of them are children of divorced parents. They are afraid of commitment and afraid to repeat their parents' mistakes. As a consequence, many people will go out on a regular basis but if the "M" word, or marriage, is brought up, well, the mere discussion of the topic may cause the couple to fight over commitment. It may even cause the couple to break up if one of them is not ready.

The Internet has changed the dating process, as on-line dating is becoming more popular with young people. There are chat rooms. What if we are in a relationship with someone we see every day and yet think we are in love with another person on the Internet? Suddenly, the vocabulary we have used for centuries doesn't quite work to describe Internet relationships.

The cell phone has also changed dating. Does a conversation count as a meeting time? What if we are talking with the person more than going out with them? The ability to reach someone anytime has made dating a less important event. Of course, we can always turn off the cell phone, which may send a message that we are upset with another person or that we want to be left alone.

Today, the bar scene is limited. Monday night is football watching night in the United States, and many men are found in front of the television screen in bars. Some women avoid bars altogether thinking that it is a place for single men who are only looking to pick up girls for sex and not a relationship.

Singles have come up with a new solution to meeting many people in a short period of time, *speed dating*. They pay $20-30 dollars and have a user name to remain anonymous and to meet many dates in one evening. For speed dating, there is a group with an equal number of men and women and usually of the same age range. The women stay at their tables and the men change seats every few minutes. In a matter of seven to ten minutes, the date can be asked just about anything except his or her age, real name, occupation and residence. The idea is to focus on what the person is really like. The dates try to get to know each other as fast as they can. Later, they can tell the agency who they have liked and the agency gives further contact information. Singles get to meet a number of people in a two-hour period. This is much more intense search for a mate than trying to do this hit and miss with one person. In this date selection process, first impressions are extremely important.

Work is a common place to meet someone, but what happens if you have chosen a female-dominated job such as nursing, teaching and social service jobs, or a male-dominated one like construction, electrical engineering, or the police force?

When we date, many expressions are used to convey the nuances of not fully committing to one person. When we flirt with someone or show we like him or her through eye contact or by dropping verbal hints, we are *"hitting on someone."* When we are physically affectionate with someone at parties and in cars, we are *"making out."* If we change our minds about a person who we were once so passionate about, we ignore him, or *"brush him off."*

Young people plan and cancel dates or *"make and break dates."* There is the *"double date"* when two couples go out together and which is less threatening for those who are unsure about the potential partner. If we want to get to know someone and don't know how to begin, we might start by *"feeding someone a line"* that goes something like, *"Haven't I met you somewhere?"*

If you meet someone at a party for the first time and later go somewhere else to get to know the person better, *"you have been picked up"* or *"you picked someone up,"* depending on who took the initiative or *"made the first move."*

"Are you a couple?" means are you boyfriend and girlfriend? *"I'm seeing someone"* does not necessarily mean that you have an exclusive sexual relationship with another person. We try to avoid promising to be faithful to someone, or at least we try hard to act unattached and free of commitment. We want to appear *"still available."*

Some Americans change girlfriends or boyfriends so often that they joke among themselves asking, *"Who is it this time?"* Many think of it as a game. If the person is not a sincere man or woman and goes out with many different people, we say, *"He's a player,"* or *"She's a player."*

Young people frequently go out with the opposite sex just for companionship and friendship in the United States. A romantic relationship is not assumed but can be sometimes questioned by others. When people ask the couple what their relationship is, a common answer is, *"We're just friends."*

Americans usually have a very romantic idea about love, but at the same time, we are cynical and distrusting of true love. We expect a lot. Some of us write exactly what we want in personal ads published in the newspaper or posted on the Internet. Anyone can see what we have to offer. We have announced our great personality and perfectly-shaped bodies, and then we tell you what we are looking for in great detail. Now if you fit the characteristics described in the paragraph, you can respond to the number in our ad and leave a message. We who have placed the ad, call or e-mail you back and you may have *"a blind date"* as a result. Seeing someone by keeping contact only through e-mail messages and never meeting the person is quite a bit like going out on a blind date.

With all of these new options for dating in the United States, genuine emotions and sincere intentions are a bit hard to come by today. How can we compete with the messages of the professional kind? You go into our drugstores and see aisles filled with greeting cards. The greeting card industry makes a lot of money from our emotions. Personally writing down our sentiments is no longer required. Similar to voice mail options and computer-generated messages, these store-bought cards do it for us. They are artificially sweet, but we buy one of these cards anyway. It's much easier than trying to reflect on our own genuine feelings.

My dear, darling, honey, sweetie, pumpkin, sweetheart, babe, we write. Any of these terms of endearment will do, as long as we begin our affectionate greeting at the top of the card before the text message. The rest is filled out for us, so we hurry down to the bottom of the card. We write as many X X X's and O O O's as we want, we sign our name on our $3.99 greeting card and we're done.

Maintaining a romantic relationship through e-mail poses a challenge today. There is often a false intimacy that comes with relationships kept alive by long-distance e-mails. Just because we are able to write a person any time does not necessarily mean our relationship is any stronger. Frequency of contact does not automatically reflect the quality of a relationship.

In the past, we received immediate feedback from a person in a face-to-face encounter. Today, feedback from other people is often reduced to a couple of words in an e-mail reply the next day, which may simply read, "good idea," or "sorry." This brief response will likely arrive in our inbox and could leave us with the feeling of "Is that all?"

Electronic communication is so common and so new, we do not really know its long-term effects on our human relationships. What is certain, however, is that by the click of a mouse, we can learn how people from other parts of the world are both different and yet alike in many ways.

Notes

"Love is temporary insanity curable by marriage."

– Ambrose Bierce
American short-story writer, (1842-1914)

A Visit to the Doctor

Chapter 21:

Ills, Pills & Medical Bills

I f you are among the countless visitors who have come to the U.S. from foreign shores, you look forward to many things – seeing the neon lights of Las Vegas, visiting the Grand Canyon, going to Disneyland or a Broadway play. Seeing a doctor wasn't in your travel plans. But now that you have every symptom in the medical book, you wonder what you're supposed to do. Should you go to the emergency room?

It isn't easy going to a doctor in a strange land. But you don't need to worry. You can be assured that: a) going to a doctor here doesn't have to be a traumatic experience; b) medical care isn't limited to the hospital emergency room. So before you decide to spend all night in an emergency room for your flu symptoms, read on to find out what you can expect at one of the U.S.' most popular attractions: the real ER.

The emergency room at 6:30 pm on a Friday afternoon. American doctors usually stop working at 5:00 pm and most don't work on weekends, so when people need a doctor at night or on the weekends, they head straight to the emergency room. In fact, a good number of visits to the emergency room are not emergencies at all, but rather, routine visits by people with limited access to health care. So you'll join the company of other strangers who are sick with the flu and bad colds – some of them wheezing, sneezing, sniffling, scratching and waiting.

You'll also be joining people who have no health insurance. They go to the nearest hospital when they are sick because emergency rooms are required by law to see all patients who enter their doors regardless of their ability to pay. Patients are seen in order of medical urgency, not in order of arrival. This means it is impossible to predict how long you'll have to wait to see a doctor. Normally, you can expect to wait several hours in the usually packed emergency room waiting area. The emergency room is sounding like a rather unpleasant way to be introduced to the U.S. health care system.

So you decide to wait until Monday to make an actual appointment to see a doctor in his or her office instead. Monday comes and you have survived the weekend. You pull out your recently purchased U.S. health insurance card for the number to call. You dial the number on the back of your card. A female voice answers and gives you a multiple choice quiz. If you want to make an appointment, press 1. If you want to speak to a nurse, press 2. If this is a life-threatening emergency, hang up and dial 911. If you want to talk to a receptionist or are calling from a rotary phone, please stay on the line and someone will be with you shortly.

You wait on the phone and press the correct buttons on the doctor's office voice mail. You finally get the human voice of the receptionist. "The next available appointment is in a two weeks," she tells you, so you take the date she offers.

Your appointment day has arrived. You don't really feel that sick anymore. However, you still have a few symptoms, so you have kept your appointment. Plus, you've already finished your suitcase full of home remedies you had brought from your country.

You step into the doctor's office and greet the receptionist with a hearty "Good afternoon." Two women are planted at the computer station. They don't look up or nod back. Instead, they are concentrating on their computer screens. One woman is wearing a headset and has a faraway look on her face. She appears to be talking to the air, but she is talking on the telephone, of course.

If this is your first visit to this doctor, you have been told on the telephone to arrive a half hour early to fill out the paperwork: You are given a two-page medical history form and an "informed consent" form, which you must sign as a promise to not sue the doctor. You also sign an HIPA, or a medical privacy act paper, that gives the doctor permission to reveal your health information to others if it's related to treatment or surgery. You have the urge to make the stack of papers into a dozen paper airplanes.

When the receptionist finally looks up, you tell her your name.

"I have a 4 o'clock appointment with the doctor," you say.

She then peels your name label off one pile of papers and sticks it on another pile.

"Insurance?" she asks.

You dig into your purse or wallet and hand it to her. She makes a photocopy of your card. She types in your medical ID number on the computer and then retrieves your medical chart.

This part of the doctor's visit is even more complicated if you carry international medical coverage from your own country. Your international health plan may not be accepted by doctors or hospitals in the United States. Most likely, you will have to pay out of your own pocket for medical expenses and then wait for reimbursement from your home-based plan. But let's say you have bought a

U.S.-based health plan, so we will continue the story of a typical visit to the doctor under that circumstance.

"Co-payment?" The receptionist gives you back your card.

You slide her a $20 bill. She scribbles you a receipt.

"Have a seat," she says in a monotone voice.

You join other seated patients, looking like ducks in a row. Magazines are stacked up on the tables. Soft pop music plays in the background.

You wait your turn. Twenty-five minutes later the nurse calls out your name like a clerk calling out your number at a New York deli. Her voice has aroused you from your near hibernation. You are taken from the waiting area into another area of the office.

"Get on the scale," the nurse orders. She weighs you. You might get lucky if the nurse tells you your weight in kilos. It's about half the number for pounds, and, fortunately, few Americans fully understand the metric system. The nurse then leads you to an examination room where she takes your blood pressure. "The doctor will be with you shortly," the nurse informs you as she closes the door and leaves you in the examination room.

You climb up on the examination table. Then you wait another 15 minutes for the doctor.

The doctor finally arrives.

"What seems to be the problem?"

You explain what has been bothering you since you made the appointment two weeks ago. If you are experiencing pain, the doctor might ask you to rate your pain on a scale of 1 to 10.

"Have you been taking any medications?" the doctor asks.

"No, but every time I... "

The doctor then asks about your family history.

Just as you are getting back to the details of your situation, the doctor tears off a piece of paper from a pad and hands it to you.

"We need a blood test."

You wanted medicine, but instead of a prescription, the doctor has ordered a laboratory test. Now you'll have to call the office to make another appointment and go to a different place in order to have the lab work done.

"The office will call you when we get the results. You can make another appointment after that." Then the doctor is gone.

Your actual visit with the doctor might have lasted 10 or 15 minutes.

An office visit similar to the one described above will likely come as a bit of a culture shock to some international visitors. It may be different from a visit to the doctor in many countries where you can show up at a medical clinic, wait for the doctor and then tell the doctor what is wrong, and get medicine from the doctor or a pharmacy the same day. In France, some doctors still make house calls. When you have an urgent need to visit a doctor in the U.S., a same-day or next-day appointment is hard to get. It normally takes one to two weeks and can even take up to a month to see a doctor. Second, the payment and the paperwork tend to be more complicated in the U.S. since not everyone has medical insurance. When you finally have managed to see the doctor, he or she may have seemed rushed, and the office visit too short. The whole experience might have seemed cold and calculated—like there were too many procedures and not enough personal attention.

From the Doctor's Point of View

Patient appointments are normally scheduled every 15 minutes in the U.S. Doctors see an average of 25 patients a day. Each visit is supposed to run like clockwork. This is because health insurance companies pay the doctor for procedures, not for compassionate conversations. It's not that doctors are greedy, but they must make enough income to meet the costs of running a medical practice and to pay for their very high insurance premiums. They are operating in a medical system where many parties are involved and getting paid. There are medical billing companies, health insurance companies, the doctors themselves, and in the case of a Medicare and Medicaid visit, the U.S. government. Several companies are employed in the process of billing and processing for private insurance, advertising, market analysis, and tracking of patients. Administrative costs are estimated to run as much as 31 percent of the total dollars spent on health care, *The New England Journal of Medicine* reported in an in-depth study of U.S. health care.

Doctors used to be right next to God in the United States in terms of prestige. But the image of a doctor in the United States has changed in the past two decades. The 1960's image of a doctor as an old, professorial type with white hair and glasses is gone. In the TV dramas of *ER* and *Gray's Anatomy,* good-looking medical interns, both male and female, face life and death situations with witty dialog and fresh-looking faces after hours in the hospital. Surgical procedures and body organs are seen close up with blood and gore like never before.

In reality, being a doctor in the U.S. today is not as glamorous as the TV portrays. In fact, American doctors today are finding their medical profession less rewarding than in the past. The Kaiser Family Foundation recently surveyed doctors nationwide and found that 87 percent of them said that the overall morale of the profession has gone down in recent years. Roughly half of the surveyed doctors said they wouldn't recommend the profession to young people thinking of entering a profession in medicine. When asked for the reason, the most common factor reported was the paperwork needed for health insurance companies. This is unfortunate because doctors have the most rigorous training and preparation among all careers. They complete roughly 10 years of college, work long hospital shifts as residents at a hospital, and normally graduate with an enormous amount of debt, owing as much as $100,000 from college loans.

That is just the beginning of their medical career. In order to set up a medical practice, doctors must buy state-of-the-art medical technology and equipment in order to compete with other physicians. Then there is the cost of insuring the doctors themselves, or medical liability insurance. U.S. doctors frequently order expensive medical tests just to have strong evidence of their diagnoses and, therefore, to reduce the possibility of being sued.

From the Patient's Point of View

Patients, for the most part, see their medical care as expensive. As a result, we act like smart shoppers. We hunt for the best doctor, the best treatment, and the best hospital. If we have something that is bothering us, we may search on Google to read about our symptoms. We are active in trying to find a diagnosis and a treatment. *"Don't just stand there, do something!"* is a common expression uttered by Americans in the face of trouble, including sickness.

Our personal medical problems are seldom discussed with others outside the family, as Americans simply do not want to talk to each other about their symptoms. If we voice our complaints, we may be perceived by others as "a fatalist," "a negative thinker," or "a complainer," which runs counter to the optimism and positive thinking that so many of us prefer. Americans generally trust that science and technology can cure us of any disease.

If the doctors can't heal us, many of us believe that we can do it ourselves with natural or drugstore remedies. That's why many Americans seek out non-conventional medical practices. These alternative treatments are called Eastern, complementary, or homeopathic medicine. Research shows that 40 percent of Americans use some form of alternative medicine, ranging from taking vitamins and going to an acupuncturist or chiropractor to getting a massage and

214 What's Up, America?

buying medicine from an herbal pharmacy instead of taking a traditional doctor-prescribed medicine. Unfortunately, these treatments are usually not available from conventional doctors, nor are they paid for by our employer-sponsored health plan. The cost often comes out of our own pockets.

What we call alternative medicine or Eastern in the U.S. is simply standard treatment in China. It is also interesting to note that in South Korea, they practice both Western conventional medicine and Eastern medicine. South Korea has Western and Eastern medical schools, Western and Eastern hospitals, and Western and Eastern doctors and medicines. In an Eastern doctor's visit, for example, the doctor might smell your breath, feel your pulse, and examine your eyes. During a Western doctor's visit, the doctor might get out his stethoscope, ask you many questions, and send you to get an X-ray.

Some Americans have home remedies too. Take chicken soup, for example. Many of us believe that homemade chicken soup has miracle-working properties if we are sick with cold symptoms. A series of popular self-help books in the U.S. reflects the idea of chicken soup as a remedy. Authors Jack Canfield and Mark Victor Hansen have compiled inspirational stories about various kinds of people overcoming obstacles in *Chicken Soup for the Soul, Chicken Soup for the Couple's Soul,* and *Chicken Soup for the Teenage Soul.*

Not only do American patients treat themselves or frequently get treatment from an alternative doctor, we are increasingly getting free medical advice offered on the radio, the Web, and TV. We watch the TV commercials advertising the latest "drug" for a chronic condition. In his book *Overdosed America,* Dr. John Abramson noted that the average American sees nine TV commercials for prescription drugs a day. If we believe the drug advertisers, it seems that we are a nation suffering from depression, arthritis, high cholesterol, irritable bowels, and insomnia.

We can even call and ask doctors on TV shows about

our health problems that we would be too embarrassed to ask our actual doctors. Magazines advise us "to do our homework" or go to a doctor's visit with written questions so we don't forget to ask what's important to us. When we actually see our doctor in person, we may go in with preconceived ideas about what the doctor should do. We may even suggest a "possible" treatment or ask for a particular medicine that we have heard about without really knowing what might work best for our condition.

Americans are not embarrassed to make an appointment to seek out a consultation or a "second opinion" from another doctor if we are faced with an operation or a major illness. From an American patient point of view, getting a second opinion is an opportunity to learn more about our condition before we make an important decision about treatment or surgery.

This is in contrast to many other countries where the doctor is rarely questioned because this would seem a challenge to his or her authority. This reflects the belief in our culture that everyone is equal, and so anyone can be questioned even if he or she holds a high position in society.

The Pills

Problems sleeping? You should take this… Digestive problems? You haven't tried this… Depressed or feeling blue? Here is an antidepressant. Indeed, there is "a pill for every ill" in the U.S. Just open our bathroom medicine chests and take a look. They are jam-packed with medicines we buy at pharmacies or at the pharmacy counter in our local supermarket. All these pills prove that when we are sick, we don't always run to the doctor first. We joke that by the time we get to see a doctor, our ailments might have already disappeared.

Our medicine cabinet tells a good part of the story, though. Not only do we buy drugstore medicines or *over-the-counter medicines* in quantity, Americans take more doctor-prescribed medicine per person than in any other country. We spend an annual average of $792 per person, according to a 2008 report by the Organization of Economic Co-operation Development (OECD), which did an analysis of pharmaceutical consumption and pricing in various countries. The same report found that the U.S., with a population of roughly 300 million and representing 5 percent of the world's 6 billion people, buys nearly half of the world's drugs.

The Drugstore

So you have finally managed to get a doctor's prescription after two office visits and a lab test. It wasn't as easy as in some countries where you can buy the medicine directly from the pharmacist. Now you are off to the drugstore with your handwritten prescription to get your medicine, which you think you rightly deserve but no longer need.

Where is the nearest pharmacy? Pharmacies do not announce themselves with a green or red cross displayed outside the store. No, in the U.S., pharmacies are hidden inside larger drugstores and supermarkets. In fact, American drugstores bear no resemblance to the English chemist shop or other European pharmacies, which are primarily medicine shops. The very name "drugstore" for a shop that sells medicines surprises people from foreign shores. Isn't "drug" the name that Americans use for their illegal recreational substances?

Indeed, American drugstores sell much more than medicines. They are part department store, part book shop, candy store, and film depot. In fact, drugstores are about as close to a general store as you can get in the United States today. Historically, drugstores served as a kind of community center and included a lunch counter, and soda fountain where teenagers could meet and order a sandwich, ice cream sodas, and sundaes.

Soda fountains started in the 1890s, and they were businesses that nicely paired with pharmacies because pharmacists knew syrups and carbonation. Back then, they were called apothecaries. The soda Coca-Cola was invented by an Atlanta pharmacist, John Pemberton, who claimed it cured many diseases. Pepsi was also a soda invented by a pharmacist, Caleb Bradham, in New Bern, North Carolina in 1893, six years later. It was originally called Brad's drink after the pharmacist's last name but was later renamed Pepsi because of the drink's ability to cure *dyspepsia* or indigestion, from which the name Pepsi came. Both Coke and Pepsi were served in a glass at a soda fountain inside the pharmacy.

Nowadays, when you drive up to your neighborhood discount drugstore, like Walgreens, and go inside, there's probably no soda fountain in sight. Most of the fountains disappeared in the 1960s to be replaced with fast food restaurants and national chain drugstores. You may find a counter where a drugstore clerk serves ice cream, though, which comes from our soda fountain tradition.

You make your way to the back of the drugstore, where all you see is a small humble counter and a pharmacist in a white coat busy doing his job of dispensing medicines.

You are new to this kind of pharmacy, so you are not sure what to do next. You are told that you must leave the prescription with the pharmacist at the "drop-off" window in order for him to "fill" or dispense it. He instructs you to come back in 20 minutes. This gives the pharmacist enough time to see if your medicine is in stock, distribute the proper dosage that the doctor prescribes, and package it for you.

What should you do in the meantime? You can twiddle your thumbs and stand around the pharmacy counter and wait. Or you can *kill time* by doing what some Americans do. First, find out if your blood pressure is low, normal, or high with the do-it-yourself blood pressure cuff next to the pharmacy counter. Then weigh yourself on the scale that usually sits next to the blood pressure equipment.

Then get lost along the way among the do-it-yourself medicine shelves, which are called *over-the-counter medicines*. These medicines are presented to you in a bewildering number of open display counters and shelves where you can see medicines, touch them, and most importantly, buy them on the spur of the moment.

You decide to browse the pain reliever, or analgesic, section. You are not going to buy anything, you tell yourself. Tylenol Regular, Extra Strength Tylenol, Advil, Motrin, Nuprin, Midol, and let's not forget the Bayer aspirin and the generic store-brand versions of all of the above. Seeing all the different varieties of pain medicine gives you a headache. Before you know it, you grab any Tylenol bottle off the nearest shelf and throw it into your basket and move on to the next section.

There you find Sominex and more than a dozen brands of sleeping pills that help you get a good night's rest. You whiz by that section. Nah, not the Slim-fast, Optifast, and other cans of liquid replacement meals; you race past and land in the cold medicines. There you stop. Your head is spinning as you read the array of labels just for one brand: Robitussin DM Max, Robitussin for a Cough, Robitussin for Chest Congestion, and Robitussin for Cough, Colds and Flu. You snap up one of those in case you get sick again.

Then you feel a sudden impulse to buy more. You pick up a bottle of Head & Shoulders shampoo, a bottle of Flintstones chewable vitamins for the kids, a tube of super-size Crest toothpaste, which is 50 percent off, and two packages of disposable Gillette razors, because it was on a special, buy-one-get-one-free deal. When you return to the pharmacy's "pick-up" window 20 minutes later to collect your medicine, you are juggling an armful of goods. You have been pulled into the drugstore's Wild West shopping spree. In the time it takes the pharmacist to type up the label and grab your package of medicine from the shelf, you buy more needless stuff. It works.

The pharmacist is now waiting for you at the cash register. While he's collecting your money, he tells you how to take the medicine and the possible side effects. "It's all written on the medicine's label, which I am putting right there in the bag," he proudly says. You reluctantly pay for your goods, peek into the shopping bag just to make absolutely sure your medicine is in there, go home, and begin treatment.

Health Insurance

So we have been to the doctor, undergone the medical tests, and gotten our prescribed medicine, how are we going to pay for it? Among all the industrialized countries, the U.S. is the only country without universal health coverage. Instead, health insurance is an optional job benefit.

Since having health insurance is a privilege, not an individual right in the U.S., companies offer health insurance to their employees as a benefit only if they work full-time. Very few companies offer this insurance to part-time employees. Many of us actually look for jobs based on whether the company offers medical insurance.

Sixty percent of us have health insurance through our employer, reports the Kaiser Family Foundation. When an employer offers medical insurance, its costs are shared by the employer and employee. Employers pay a certain amount by belonging to a group plan, and they receive a tax benefit from this. At the same time, employees pay a certain amount of money (a premium), which is taken out of each monthly paycheck. In addition, we usually pay a fee, or co-payment, from our own pockets each time we see a doctor. These co-payments range from $10 to $60.

If we get sick or need an operation, the treatment or procedure is paid for from the collected premiums of other workers. If we have an accident and go to the

hospital without health insurance, it will cost more than
$1,000 dollars a day of our own money. It's no wonder that
hospitalization is a major reason Americans are not able to
afford their medical bills and is one of the most common
causes of personal bankruptcy in the U.S.

More than half of all Americans have what is called a
managed care plan for health insurance. These managed
health care plans are identified by their initials or acronym.
The two most common are the health maintenance
organizations, or HMOs, and the preferred provider
organizations, or PPOs.

If we belong to an HMO, we are limited in our choice
of which doctor we can see. We must go to a primary
doctor called a PCP (primary care provider) who belongs
to a group practice (a network) that is associated with our
employer's health insurance plan.

With an HMO plan, we must ask our primary doctor
for a referral in order to see a specialist. Then we have to
wait a couple of weeks longer until the primary doctor's
referral to the specialist is approved by our health insurance
plan. Only then are we able to make the appointment with
a specialist. In other words, those of us with HMO plans
need to make several doctor appointments in order to
get specialized care for our condition. HMOs have been
criticized for denying or delaying needed care because
of the time it takes to get the permission for treatment. It
may take weeks or even months before the patient and the
doctor are granted permission from the health insurance
company for the proper medical procedures. The patient
must wait before receiving care, and the doctor will not
continue treatment until he or she is assured that the health
insurance company will pay for the whole medical care
process.

A PPO has fewer restrictions. Unlike an HMO, you
can choose your own doctor with this kind of plan.
However, you must pay for your own medical expenses
up to a certain amount of money (a deductible) before

your insurance company begins to pay your medical bills. The advantage of a PPO plan is that it allows you to go directly to a specialist without having to get a referral from a primary care doctor.

A sizeable number of Americans, 47 million people or 16 percent of our population, have no health insurance. In a weak labor market, workers may lose their jobs or be forced to take jobs without benefits, thus losing their employer-provided health insurance. This is why the number of people without health insurance in the U.S. is increasing.

The U.S. government does, however, pay for health insurance for certain segments of the population. Senior citizens and the disabled, for example, have a government plan called Medicare. Low-income families have a government plan called Medicaid. Individuals on these two government plans make up 27 percent of the total number of Americans that have health insurance. Some people on government plans may have been counted twice though, because it's possible to have two types of health insurance: one that you may have qualified for when you became a senior citizen, the other one through your employer after you retired. The federal government also pays for health insurance for military personnel called Tricare. Military veterans even have special hospitals where they can go for their medical care called Veterans Affairs Hospitals or VA hospitals.

Comparing Our Health Care to Other Nations

Compared with other industrialized countries, the U.S. consistently ranks poorly in measurements of the population's health and medical care experiences. In fact, the United States placed last among 19 industrialized countries when it came to preventable deaths such as treatable cancers, diabetes, and cardiovascular disease in a 2008 Commonwealth Fund-supported report on the quality of health care. Researchers Ellen Nolte and Martin McKee of the London School of Hygiene and Tropical Medicine tracked deaths that were preventable by access to timely and effective health care, and researchers estimated over 100,000 deaths per year could be prevented in the U.S., which points to a major weakness in our nation's health care system.

It may come as a surprise that our country lags behind others in quality and access because we spend twice as much per person than any other developed country on health care, an average of $8,000 per person. Today, the United States devotes 16 percent of its gross domestic product to medical care.

Why? The reasons for the poor showing of our health care system are too complex to cover in this guide, but one fundamental problem in U.S. health care is the way our medical system is centered on hospitals rather than preventive care. We wait for people to get sick and then spend enormous amounts of money to heal them or to prolong life in its final stages. Doctors who specialize make much more money than family practitioners, so fewer and fewer doctors want to become primary care physicians in the U.S. In fact, more than half of our doctors are specialists, which is more than in any other country.

Looking for Medical Care Abroad

As costs for health care continue to grow, Americans are going overseas in increasing numbers in search of less expensive treatments and surgeries. An estimated 1.5 million U.S. citizens will seek health care outside the U.S. in 2008, reports Deloitte Consulting Company, which tracks American medical tourists. The growth in medical tourism has the potential to cost U.S. health care providers billions of dollars in lost revenue.

Major centers for medical tourism are Bangkok and Phuket, Thailand. Six medical facilities in Bangkok alone have received hospital accreditation from the United

States by the Joint Commission International (JCI), the international arm of the organization that reviews and accredits American hospitals. India has also become a major player in medical tourism through the Apollo Group, its largest hospital group. These hospitals in Asia are like luxury hotels, offering such amenities as barbers and hair salons, as well as non-urgent procedures like plastic surgery.

In addition, prominent U.S. medical schools are opening foreign branches. Harvard Medical School has partnered with hospitals in Mumbai, India, and with the Dubai Healthcare City in the United Arab Emirates. Singapore's major hospitals have partnered with Johns Hopkins University in Baltimore.

The Future: Universal Coverage?

Try talking to any American about their health care. He or she will tell you that they are very proud of the competence of our doctors, the specialized medical treatments, and the access to sophisticated operations. They will probably say, "We have the best medical care in the world."

At the same time, most of us believe that the health care system needs major reform. Ninety percent of Americans consistently believe that the U.S. health care system should be completely rebuilt or fundamentally changed, reports *The New England Journal of Medicine*, which analyzed surveys conducted from 1991 to 2007 by *The New York Times* and *CBS News*.

American medicine is a classic paradox. It offers the best medicine a country can offer while at the same time, not offering health care to 16 percent of its people.

Though Americans agree that we need to change our current health system, we have a much harder time agreeing on how to fix it. When politicians propose that the U.S. government get more involved, the debate brings up the politically charged concept of "socialized medicine." This term often causes fear in many people who view it as government interference in private enterprise and reject government proposals. The political debate on health care reform tends to center on who will pay for the reforms and how will health care be administered. Should we have a government-paid system or a system paid for by private companies or a public-private partnership?

In the near future, we may implement a universal health care system that would cover every single American regardless of their age, employment, or wealth. If we achieve this, then our country will be the last of the industrialized nations to do so.

Notes

"Only in America – do drugstores make the sick walk all the way to the back of the store to get their prescriptions while healthy people can buy cigarettes at the front of the store."

– Anonymous

A Game for All Seasons

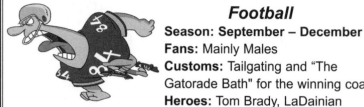

Football
Season: September – December
Fans: Mainly Males
Customs: Tailgating and "The Gatorade Bath" for the winning coach
Heroes: Tom Brady, LaDainian Tomlinson, and Peyton Manning
Hall of Fame: Canton, OH

Basketball
Season: December – May
Fans: Males and Females
Customs: Cheerleaders
Heroes: LeBron James, Kobe Bryant, Shaquille O'Neal & Yao Ming
Hall of Fame: Springfield, MA

Baseball
Season: March – October
Fans: Families
Customs: 7th inning stretch and the song "Take Me Out to the Ballgame"
Heroes: Sammy Sosa, Barry Bonds, Manny Ramirez and Mark McGuire
Hall of Fame: Cooperstown, NY

Ice Hockey
Season: October – April
Fans: Mostly Males
Customs: "A Hat Trick"
Heroes: Wayne Gretsky (Canadian) & Alex Ovechkin, (Russian)
Hall of Fame: Toronto, Canada

Chapter 22:

A Game for All Seasons

I t's hard to imagine, but the lowly baseball cap started out as a simple means for protecting baseball players from the sun. Now the cap is worn by football fans, golfers, and tennis players alike. Spike Lee, Steven Spielberg, and Michael Moore all wear a baseball cap. Even the Dalai Lama wore a baseball cap during his 2008 visit to Washington, D.C.

You don't have to be an American to wear one, but you might feel kind of American when you do. That is, when you're feeling casual and young at heart. You can put on a cap any which way: forwards, backwards, or sideways. Your favorite team's logo can be embroidered on it, but it really doesn't have to be your favorite team at all. Actually, you might not know anything about American football or baseball; it just has to be the name of a U.S. sports team.

So let's say you are wearing your cap just because you feel like it. You are new to the United States, and you only know about soccer, which is known as football by most of the world. If anyone were to ask, "Are you going to watch the game today?" simply reply, "Which game?" More than likely, on any given day, a game is being played somewhere in the United States. It could be a Friday night high school football game, a Saturday night college football game, or a Sunday professional football game. With four major professional sports: football, basketball, baseball, and ice hockey, it's common to have two or more sports playing at the same time.

Take October, for example, which is football season. The professional baseball teams are finishing their season with a best-of-seven playoff series followed by the best-of-seven World Series championship. So in addition to football being televised every weekend and many weekday nights, you will also see a lot of baseball on TV in October.

This is the essence of understanding American sports culture. We spend a lot of our time watching endless sports events on TV. More than likely, if it's a Saturday or Sunday, a great number of us will be home watching "the game."

Most of the games are free to watch. Television developed alongside the professional leagues in the U.S. and has even changed the nature of American games. First, there is the sheer quantity of games televised on the four major networks – CBS, NBC, ABC, and FOX – which broadcast regular season games free of charge. This is in addition to the ESPN family of 24-hour sports channels and the many regional sports networks (RSNs) for which we must subscribe to cable or satellite TV services to receive. This has created the phenomenon of *football widows,* which is a term often used to describe mainly females whose partners watch a great deal of football on television and ignore their relationships.

You will see dozens of commercials during any televised game here. When the timeouts are called in a football or basketball game, the TV channel inserts the advertisers' commercials that pay for the broadcast of the games. The 16-game NFL season has been around since 1978, but the broadcast coverage has greatly expanded in recent years. Some people believe it has grown just to generate more television revenue.

The sports event of the year is (drum roll, please) the Super Bowl, the battle waged between the best two football teams of the year. It's a giant tribal gathering in the U.S. We sit in front of our giant screens. We invite friends over to share giant bowls of chips and order pizza for Super Bowl parties. We don't only watch the Super Bowl. We take part in it. We watch the National Football League's game as if we were sitting in an ancient Roman Coliseum watching our gladiators grunt and push and pound each other until they fall to the ground. Isn't it amazing how the quarterback is hurt but continues to play? Now, that's the Roman spirit. We even use Roman numerals to identify the final football game, rather than the year it was held. For example, Super Bowl XLIII, played on February 1, 2009, was for the 2008 season.

Nearly half of the U.S. population watches the Super Bowl. Even Americans who normally don't watch football often view the game because of its creative commercials and its halftime entertainment, which is on a huge scale. Famous bands and singers perform, like the Rolling Stones and Bruce Springsteen. We comment on how well the national anthem was sung or "performed."

Why do we sing the *"Oh say, can you see"* song at sporting events, anyway? That custom began when many baseball players were accused of being "unpatriotic" during World War I (1914–1918) by playing professional baseball in order to avoid serving in the military. To demonstrate their patriotism, baseball players began to sing the national anthem before the game to show their fans that they, indeed, loved their country. Soon, the national anthem spread to other sports and is now sung at most major U.S. sporting events. It wasn't until 1968, however, that pop stars began to sing their own personal interpretations of the national anthem. Puerto Rican singer Jose Feliciano was the first to give his personal interpretation to our national song at the

1968 World Series in Detroit. When Feliciano strummed his guitar in a blues style and sang the national anthem in his own way, it shocked many people and caused an uproar among fans who questioned his patriotism.

At the end of the football game, especially a championship game like the Super Bowl, the winning team's players take a water cooler full of a sports drink called *Gatorade* and pour it all over the winning coach, giving him a "Gatorade Bath." The *Gatorade* stains the coach's clothes red and marks him with victory.

Our Athletic Presidents

Ever since President William Howard Taft threw out the first pitch to start the professional baseball season in 1910 in Washington, D.C., sports and presidents have gone together in the U.S. like macaroni and cheese. Who would remember that Taft, at 350 pounds (160 kilos), once got stuck in a White House bath tub and needed six aides and a gallon of butter to get out? It was the tradition of throwing the "first ceremonial pitch" to signal Opening Day of the baseball season that counted in history. Eleven U.S. presidents have done the same since that first day in 1910.

The fact that we follow our presidents as they privately practice a sport is proof that we greatly admire physical strength in our culture. Newspapers often print pictures of our presidents running, golfing, or biking. They are sometimes photographed in their sweat suits on their way to go running for exercise. When they come out of the gym or are done practicing their sport, they are all sweaty, but they are still friendly enough to shake the hands of onlookers. They seem to always wear a baseball cap when they practice their sport so that they appear to be ordinary guys, "just one of us."

President Barack Obama plays basketball, and he's a Chicago White Sox fan. Among former presidents, George

W. Bush owned the Texas Rangers baseball team. He also rode his mountain bike for exercise while in office. Bill Clinton ran and played golf. George H. Bush was the captain of his Yale baseball team. Gerald Ford played football at the University of Michigan. The list goes on and on about our athletic presidents. But no one can beat Teddy Roosevelt for being the most athletic of all presidents.

Roosevelt climbed the Matterhorn, led an African safari, and explored the Amazon jungle. On one of his hunting trips in 1902, Roosevelt refused to shoot a bear cub, calling it unsportsmanlike. Because of this hunting adventure, a toy store owner created a little bear and named it after the president; thus, we have the "Teddy Bear." Roosevelt also created the organization that regulates college sports, the National Collegiate Athletic Association (NCAA), in 1910. He sought to organize the various college presidents to do something about the growing number of serious injuries and deaths in college football at the time.

The Wide World of American Sports

Professional U.S. basketball, baseball, and soccer leagues have attracted a growing number of foreign athletes and fans. As a result, our locally-based home teams are looking a lot more like international teams. Many young international fans have been introduced to U.S. professional league games through the NBA, NFL, NHL, and MLB video games and online fantasy league games. U.S. games are more accessible online as sports broadcasting has expanded abroad. Since the U.S. has established developmental basketball, baseball, and American football teams and programs abroad, many international players have come to the United States to play. International players seek to play on U.S. teams for the public exposure, higher level of competition, and, of course, the million-dollar contracts.

Basketball has been quickly spreading to other

countries in the past two decades. Michael Jordan was instrumental in globalizing the sport by his international appeal as a star athlete. Then the fast food giant McDonald's started sponsoring international basketball tournaments in 1987, which brought an NBA team to play against the best basketball teams in Spain, Italy, Russia, and Greece. After that, "The Dream Team" of Michael Jordan, Magic Johnson, and Larry Bird was put together. This famous U.S. team played for the 1992 Barcelona Olympic Games, watched by millions of people around the world. Today, the NBA plays some pre-season games and a few regular season games abroad. Yao Ming plays a key role in capturing the hearts of Chinese fans while he plays for the Houston Rockets.

Baseball has taken a different course than basketball. Though interest in this sport may be declining in the United States, its popularity is as strong as ever in Venezuela, Cuba, and the Dominican Republic as well as in Japan, South Korea, and Taiwan.

This was not always the case. Ever since the first "World Series" in 1903, major league baseball's championship round has always been between two American teams rather than two international teams as the name "World" would seem to imply. Few non-U.S. baseball teams existed over 100 years ago. In fact, in countries where baseball is now firmly planted as a sport, such as in Japan, Korea, Taiwan, the Caribbean, and Venezuela, U.S. military troops had often introduced the game to the host country when stationed there. Some of our American religious missionaries exported it as well, as was the case when baseball was introduced to South Korea.

A little over 100 years later, in March 2006, the first truly "World" professional baseball tournament was played outside the Olympic Games. Japan beat Cuba in the 16-nation competition, winning the first ever World Baseball Classic. Two years later, South Korea won the gold medal at the 2008 Summer Olympics in Beijing, beating the same Cuban team. In March 2009, both Japan and South Korea dominated the international baseball competition again with Japan winning its second straight World Baseball Classic title.

Globalizing American football has been harder to do than it has been for basketball and baseball. The NFL Europe League operated in Europe for 16 years and was a major part of the NFL's strategy to develop and test new talent as well as internationalize American football. The European League struggled for fans and lost money over time, and ultimately the NFL Europe League closed in 2007. The United States has also started a smaller program called the *USA Football International Student Programs,* which gives international students a chance to play football and study at prestigious U.S. prep schools. For the 2008-2009 school year, 12 students from three continents were invited to participate in this program.

Ice hockey has always been popular in U.S. states that share a border with Canada. Actually, the National Hockey League is really a Canadian-U.S. league despite the "National" in its name. Canada dominated this winter sport and had the strongest NHL hockey teams for over 100 years. Then in the 1990s, teams based in American cities (often featuring Canadian-born players) started beating Canadian teams for the Stanley Cup. Though the sport of ice hockey may never enjoy the popularity that pro football, basketball, and baseball do in the U.S., American hockey fans are very loyal. Actually, they are often *diehard* or *hardcore* fans, which are fans in any sport who support their teams whether they win or lose. In contrast, fans who only show their support to a team when it is doing well are called *fair-weather* fans. Internationally, ice hockey has also enjoyed a large fan base in cold-weather countries such as Sweden, Finland, and Norway. Of course, there are many people in Russia and Eastern Europe who are also big hockey fans.

For professional soccer games featuring Mexico's national and club teams, stadiums are often packed with fans of Mexican heritage. Our southern neighbor plays many games in the United States and has a very loyal following of fans from Mexico.

Since American teams operate as franchises, professional players are either traded or they can look for another team to join as "free agents" after their existing contract expires. Every year, a U.S. team changes at least a few players, so it's hard to follow exactly who is playing on which team. As of press time, here is a sampling of the international players playing on U.S. pro teams.

In Major League Baseball, we have Japanese players such as Ichiro Suzuki of the Seattle Mariners, Daisuke Matsuzaka for the Boston Red Sox, and Hideki Matsui of the New York Yankees; Cuban pitchers, who are half-brothers, Liván Hernández of the Minnesota Twins and Orlando ("El Duque") Hernández of the New York Mets; Taiwanese pitcher Chien-Ming Wang plays for the New York Yankees; Ching-Lung Hu is a shortstop with the Los Angeles Dodgers; and Korean pitcher Chan Ho Park is currently with the Philadelphia Phillies. Sammy Sosa is just one of dozens of stars from the Dominican Republic who have made their mark on Major League Baseball with an outstanding baseball career. Notable Dominican baseball players on MLB teams include Albert Pujols of the St. Louis Cardinals, Manny Ramirez of the Los Angeles Dodgers, and Alex Rodriguez who plays for the New York Yankees.

For ice hockey, Nicklas Lidstrum of Sweden became the first European-born and trained captain of an NHL team, the Detroit Red Wings. Notable Russians Evgeni Malkin plays for the Pittsburgh Penguins and Russian top scorer Alexander Ovechkin plays on the Washington Capitals.

In men's basketball, we have the aforementioned Chinese center Yao Ming of the Houston Rockets, the high-scoring forward Dirk Nowitzki from Germany on the Dallas Mavericks, and Andrea Bargnani from Italy who plays for the Toronto Raptors, to name just a few international players on NBA teams.

For the Women's National Basketball Association, or WNBA, we also have international players, such as Brazilian Janeth Arcain, who played many years for the Houston Comets from 1997 to 2005. Other international players include Brazilian Kelly Santos and Australian Lauren Jackson, who both play for the Seattle Storm, Russian Svetlana Abrosimova, who plays for the Connecticut Sun, and Pole Margo Dydek of the Los Angeles Sparks.

Today the cultural exchange goes both ways. Some of our American basketball players are heading overseas because of the National Basketball Association's 2007 rule that says basketball players must be 19 years or older or they must wait one year after high school to be drafted into the NBA. One top high school basketball player refused to wait. Brandon Jennings, a top-ranked U.S. high school basketball player, signed a $1.2 million contract to play for Italy rather than play at a U.S. college. Another American basketball player, Josh Childress, left his NBA team to play and make more money in Europe. Childress left the Atlanta Hawks in 2008 to sign a $20 million contract to play for the Greek club Olympiacos for three years in Athens.

Girls Got Game

American women have excelled in professional sports, especially in basketball and soccer. Women started playing basketball at roughly the same time as men in the United States. Only a year after Dr. James Naismith invented the game of basketball for men and the YMCA in 1891, gym instructor Senda Berenson adapted the rules for women and introduced the game to her students at Smith College. The first women's basketball game was played in 1893 at Smith College between freshman and sophomore players. At the 2008 Beijing Olympics, the U.S. women's basketball team became the first women's traditional team sport to win four straight gold medals.

The U.S. women's national soccer team is very strong,

too. They won three of the last four Olympic gold medals in soccer. Since 2000, women in the U.S. have also had a professional football league and, since 1998, a professional hockey league.

Though women have professional leagues in all four major team sports, female coaches, umpires, and referees in professional games are still rare. Television coverage of women's pro sports also lags behind coverage of men's pro sports.

Why Not "Soccer"?

Why do Americans call the sport "soccer" when most of the world calls it "football"? The word "soccer" allegedly came into use when an Englishman made a nickname out of the formal name "Association Football." Since the game of rugby was already called "rugger" at the time, Charles Wreford Brown, an Oxford University student, shortened the word "association" by dropping the first letter *a*, shortening it to "socca" and then adding "er" to end up with what we call "soccer" today.

One of the top reasons Americans give for not following soccer is that we already have four professional sports to choose from: American football, basketball, baseball, and ice hockey. Three of the four professional sports were invented here: baseball, basketball, and American football. In fact, eight of our largest cities have at least one team in each of the four sports. Only Los Angeles lacks four sports; it doesn't have a professional football team.

Soccer critics also say Americans like games with high scores. In American football games, each team's score is often in the 20 to 30 point range, and in baseball, it can be from 1 to 10, while a basketball game can easily reach 100 points for each team. In contrast, soccer scores of 2-0 or 3-1 seem relatively low.

Soccer games end in ties. This is impossible in basketball and baseball because the two teams play overtime periods until someone scores. As if we need more proof that we like a clear winner or loser for our teams, hockey changed its rules in the 2005–2006 season so that games can no longer end in a tie as they could in the past. Now, ice hockey games must go to an overtime shootout until there is a winner.

Changing Americans' mind about the world's most loved sport won't be easy. Hosting the 1994 World Cup was one attempt. Another attempt to attract more fans to the sport has been to bring English soccer player David Beckham to the U.S. in 2007 to play on the Los Angeles Galaxy. However, only time will tell if having a star player on a Major League Soccer team will help draw more fans to soccer, because it is uncertain how long Beckham will even play in the U.S.

All these objections to soccer are looked upon with a degree of suspicion by international visitors. Many soccer fans from other countries believe that Americans don't like following soccer because the U.S. league does not excel in this sport. International visitors have said that Americans won't ever like the sport in which their teams won't rank as one of the top teams. When Americans defend themselves by saying that our soccer teams are still relatively new and the U.S. is developing top players, or that females and young people increasingly play the sport, many international visitors view this as an excuse.

Going to a Game

Let's suppose that as an international visitor, you decide to go to an American football game to see "what all the noise is about." You might still have hard feelings toward Americans because of all the bad things they have said about your beloved soccer, but you decide to give the American game a second chance.

So you set off to find a Ticketmaster outlet. You want to buy a ticket for a home game, you tell the clerk at the ticket window. "Cheapest tickets, $89," the clerk replies. You discover that going to a pro game costs as much as seeing a Broadway show or a rock concert in the United States. For a good seat at any of these games, you can easily pay more than $100 for a ticket, which would get you into the lower stands to see the game close-up. If you want the cheapest seat in the place, you can always bring your binoculars.

You hear that going to a pro baseball game is a bit more affordable because it is considered a family event. Prices usually start at around $15 a seat. However, there are plenty of high-priced tickets for better seats, too. No wonder many U.S. fans complain about the high ticket prices. Many people blame it on the professional players whose average salary is about $2.9 million, though player salaries range from a minimum of $300,000 for backup players to $20 million for stars.

"What kind of ticket are you going to buy?" the clerk is asking you, waiting impatiently. You're still thinking it over. "Tickets are going fast," the ticket clerk tells you. Tickets go on sale months ahead in the U.S. rather than weeks ahead as in other countries. Some fans buy tickets for all the home games, or "season tickets." Corporations often buy a group of game tickets to give to employees and clients as gifts or rewards. Real estate agents have been known to give away tickets to families who buy a home through them.

You finally decide on a ticket for $89. You can see the guy waiting in line behind you is relieved. He had his wallet out and has been ready to pay since you've been there.

The clerk gives you the ticket. It's for an assigned seat. There are no tickets for general access to a particular section of the stadium. This is unlike in Europe, where you can buy a ticket to stand up anywhere within the section to watch a soccer match. You are learning that an American football game comes with a whole new set of rules.

No one asked you at the ticket office what side you were cheering for, either. In Brazil and Italy, for example, you have to ask the ticket clerk for a specific side, because the home team and the visiting team enter through separate entrances to avoid any possible confrontation with the fans of the rival team.

Game day finally arrives, and you find your seat is in the upper rows. Strange, but you are sitting next to a man who is wearing the rival team's jersey. You realize that there aren't separate stands for fans of the home team and the visiting team. Despite the mixed-seating arrangement, it doesn't seem dangerous. There are security officers everywhere. You have been told that the worst that could happen is that a fan who had too much to drink might accidentally spill beer on the back of your shirt. Even so, you don't want that to happen.

Fans have arrived incredibly early at the stadium. You arrived an hour before the game, and you thought you would be one of the first ones there. When you parked your car in the stadium's parking lot, it was nearly full. Plenty of fans had already unloaded tables and chairs from their trunks and had their barbecues set up. The trash containers overflowed with empty beer cans. It seemed like some of them had already eaten their grilled hot dogs and hamburgers and had consumed plenty of drinks. Odd, but why are these fans celebrating *before* the game? Oh, yes, these people have a special name in the U.S. They are called *tailgaters*.

After you are settled inside the stadium, you have a chance to look around. The first thing you notice about the atmosphere is that it's noisy. It's much too loud to have much of a conversation with the man sitting next to you during the game. The sound system has been turned up so high that it is more like an attack on all your senses, especially your sense of hearing.

The football game has started. All is relatively calm on the part of the fans. American fans tend to cheer as they

The Super Bowl

"Hey, did I miss the commercials?"

The Super Bowl is a major televised sports event held in January or February.

Fans watch the professional championship game on TV together with friends and family. They talk about how the national anthem is sung, watch the year's best commercials, and enjoy the halftime show with stars like The Rolling Stones and Prince.

Our Favorite Sport to Watch

Football – far more than any other sport. A 2008 Gallup poll found that 41% of Americans watch football on TV, 10% watch baseball, 9% watch basketball, 4% ice hockey. Only 3% watch soccer.

Tailgate Parties

On game day, fans get to the stadium early to find a good parking spot where they can "set up camp."

They open their truck's "tailgate" (or the trunk of their car) and unpack hamburgers, coolers and a grill to have a barbecue and enjoy a pre-game party in the parking lot.

follow the plays in the game. In contrast, Europeans often sing fan songs during the entire soccer match because the game is perceived less as a "show" and more as a "war" between teams. Insults are shouted at the opposing team.

The relatively calm fan behavior seen at the game might be due to the fact that American football teams mostly play against other U.S. and Canadian teams throughout the year. This is unlike soccer teams in many countries. Soccer teams compete not only within their internal national league, but their national teams also compete against other countries in a regional cup tournament every year. Soccer as a sport is a unifier, representing one's country playing against another country. It follows then that a sports event becomes a patriotic event where one nation stands up against another and decides who is better.

Rock music and old disco tunes blare from the stadium's speakers. Each stadium has a play list of songs that tend to be the same ones heard at every other major sports event. The typical "jock rock" includes the Black Eyed Peas' "Let's Get It Started," the Village People's "YMCA," and Queen's "We Will Rock You." The public address system also dominates the game. The announcer tells you when to clap your hands. You read messages on the video screens that instruct you to "Make Some Noise," which takes away from some of the spontaneity of going to a live game.

You've been told that watching a live ice hockey game in the U.S., though, is an entirely different matter for both fans and players alike. Despite the protective barriers, announcers warn fans to look out for flying pucks, and a warning is written on the back of the ticket. The fastest of all team sports, ice hockey has been described as a combination of "blood, sweat, and beauty." Fans are likely to see "goons," or hockey players whose role is to get into fights with players from the rival team. It can be brutal to watch a player get hit in the face with a hockey stick. Though referees give players stiff penalties for fighting, it is still common to see punches thrown among hockey players. Some fans even go to games hoping to see a fistfight break out, saying that a fight adds to the excitement of the game.

Fans behave in another unique way at hockey games: if a hockey player scores three goals in one game, called a "hat trick," which is very hard to do, fans throw their hats on the ice rink in appreciation of the outstanding player's skills. In addition to hats and caps being thrown onto the ice, other local traditions survive as well. In Detroit, Red Wings fans throw boiled octopuses on the ice rink. Fans of the Florida Panthers used to throw rubber rats on the ice rink until it was banned by the NHL. Both of these customs originated from a personal story of one of the team's players in which the octopus and rat had brought the player good luck.

Suddenly, a man next to you howls in your ear, "Touchdown!" and your mind is back at the football game you are watching. You are still trying to figure out the strategy of the game. As an outsider, it looks like two teams playing a game of chess. One calculated play after another, with players moving slowly down the giant field. Then come sudden bursts of energy. It's nearing the end of the game. A few fans can be seen leaving the game early to avoid the after-game traffic. You wait until the game is finished. In your country, if your team does poorly and loses, fans stay to confront players or coaches. If your team wins, fans tend to stay and celebrate their team's win *after* the game. In Brazil and Mexico, for example, fans might take to the streets to celebrate in public. American fans normally get into their cars and drive home. On the way home, fans honk their horns at you as they drive past to share the excitement of their team's win.

The Anatomy of a Cheerleader

Why are there mainly girls dressed in sexy clothes cheering from the sidelines of professional sporting events?

Cheerleaders primarily serve as entertainment during the games in the U.S. Ironically, cheerleading started over 100 years ago at a college football game as a male activity. Johnny Campbell, a college student, organized the crowds to cheer on his University of Minnesota team in 1898. In the early years, cheerleaders used megaphones to yell and encourage the crowds, so they were known by various names such as "yell leaders," "rooter kings," and "yell masters." In fact, George W. Bush was the head cheerleader at his high school, Phillips Academy in Andover, Massachusetts.

Females began joining the squad in 1923. That's when gymnastics, stunts, and tumbling started, and the rigorous activity continues today. In the pro leagues, cheerleaders are still mainly women, but males make up 50 percent of the cheerleading squads in colleges.

Cheerleading has spread to other countries in the last several years. South Korea and Japan now have cheerleaders leading fans in chants for both soccer and baseball games. These are two sports that we don't have cheerleaders for. Using cheerleaders in a unique cultural way, Japan presented cheerleaders at a pep rally designed for university students about to enter the job market. Teams of cheerleaders led the job hunters in chants to get them excited about searching for a job in an increasingly tight job market.

Fans Who Stay Home

A number of American sports fans these days prefer to stay home and watch the game for free. Half of U.S. sports fans believe that watching a game in high-definition television is "almost as good" as watching in person, according to a January 2008 survey by the Consumer Electronics Association and the Sports Video Group. American fans like the sportscasters' commentary, the graphics, and the biographical and statistical information about the players that a televised game provides. So for many Americans, "the best seat in the house" may be in the living room and not at the stadium.

To compete, stadiums are now starting to bring the living room to the game. New stadiums being built for the NFL are including high-definition flat-screen televisions to meet their fans' desire for constant statistical data about the players and the games. For example, the new Dallas Cowboys' stadium will feature a high-definition screen that will extend more than half the length of the field. The stadium being built for the New York Jets and Giants, which is scheduled to open in 2010, will have giant video screens in each corner, 20 video boards outside the stadium aimed at tailgaters, and more than 2,000 high-definition flat-screen televisions inside. Indeed, for American fans who love technology integrated into their games, getting a good seat has lost some of its importance. Today, many young people also like to watch mobile feeds of the game on the Internet.

Sports as a Family Affair

The whole American family usually gets involved if their children are on a sports team. Mothers spend a good part of their days picking up and dropping off their children for practice sessions and games. They are nicknamed *soccer moms, hockey moms,* and *basketball moms* after the sport their kids play. Dads volunteer to be the unpaid coaches for the community leagues. Moms and dads spend a great number of Saturday mornings watching their kids' games. The enormous commitment that American parents make in order to have their kids participate in athletics reflects their positive attitude toward sports.

Why are many parents eager to have their children join a team? American parents usually believe playing sports teaches kids good values while helping them develop discipline and social skills. Parents also like the fact that their children will benefit from the physical conditioning of a sport. It's an organized activity with adult supervision. Parents announce their children have joined a sports team and often say, "It will keep them out of trouble." This usually means sports take up so much of their children's time that kids will have no time left for other pursuits that parents are afraid of, such as experimenting with drugs or spending too much time playing video games.

Both girls and boys are encouraged by their parents to sign up to play a sport at an early age. Children as young as four or five years old can sign up for teams in "pee-wee leagues." Young boys might start out by joining a community-based baseball team called T-ball or Little League.

Sports Inside American Schools

Question: What does playing sports have to do with institutions of learning? In the United States, just about everything. Schools have their own sports teams starting in elementary school and going all the way through college. Schools all have special *school colors* to represent their sports teams. They also have a *school mascot*, which is a person, animal, or object believed to bring good luck and used as a symbol for a sports team. Tigers, bears, and lions are common animals chosen for their bravery, power, and speed. There still remains a huge controversy over Native American mascots and nicknames being used by some school and professional teams. Nicknames such as Chiefs, Blackhawks, Braves, Indians, and Redskins are considered by most Native Americans as disrespectful and offensive. Some schools and professional league teams have stopped using them entirely in recent years or have changed how they are portrayed in the mascot's costume and team logo.

Student enthusiasm or *school spirit* for their sports teams and athletes is encouraged in the schools through events called *pep rallies* in the school gymnasium. This is

Football Customs in School

Homecoming Day

This is a day full of activities mostly centered around a football game. The origin of this annual event was to welcome alumni or former students back to their school.

Spirit week – Students dress in clothing with their school's name, or their school colors the week before homecoming.

Pep rallies – The whole school meets in the gym to "boost" or encourage the spirit of the team. Team players are announced and come out in uniform. Cheerleaders lead the school in chants for their football team.

Homecoming Parade

The school has a parade with a marching band and floats created by classes and school clubs. The Homecoming Queen and King is crowned, followed by a football game.

The Homecoming Dance – It's a rather formal dance where the gym is decorated and people dance to music from a live band or a disc jockey.

where the entire school gathers with the cheerleaders to cheer and chant and sing fight songs as the players are introduced to students the day before the game.

The homecoming game is one of the most important sporting events of the year in high school and college. It is a school football game that is part of a week-long event in the fall to welcome former students back to the school. On the day before the game, there is a huge pep rally. Then there is usually a parade with floats and the school's marching band on homecoming day. The homecoming queen and king, a couple chosen from the senior class, are formally announced. The school football game is played after the parade, and at night, students get dressed up and go to a formal homecoming dance.

What sports are common to play in elementary school? Boys might join a soccer team at their school and young girls typically start playing soccer or volleyball as their first organized sport in school.

In junior high school, many American boys switch from playing soccer to playing American flag football, a game like American football in which players tear off small pieces of cloth called flags from around other players' waists instead of knocking them down. Young boys are encouraged to eventually play tackle football, though, where you knock players down to the ground or tackle them. Many parents think American football makes their boys more masculine. Some American parents see the rough game as a rite of passage into manhood and that "football turns boys into men."

Soccer has developed as a strong girl's sport in the United States because size, weight, and height are less of an issue than in American football and basketball. A 1972 federal law called Title IX forced public schools to spend an equal amount of money in education and sports for women as they did for men. At that time, only one in 27 girls participated in sports in high school. More than three decades years later, one in three girls participates in high school sports according to the Women's Sports Federation, an advocacy group that keeps track of women's participation in sports.

High School Competition and Making the Pros

Coaches push their high school teams to compete at a much higher level than in elementary and junior high. Only the best athletes are chosen because a great deal of importance is placed on winning. High school coaches become focused on training their teams intensely with hopes of going to the state championship game. As a result, these teams act as minor-league training grounds. High school games become showcases for players to demonstrate their skills to recruiters who scout them out for college teams.

Maintaining good grades in high school is often secondary to winning games for the school. The 2005 movie *Coach Carter* shows this reality. It's based on a true story of how the coach of a high school basketball team in northern California fought to raise the academic standards of an inner city team. The movie recreates Coach Ken Carter's actual experience coaching the Richmond High School basketball team, the Oilers. Because his basketball players were not taking their academic studies seriously, he locked the gym for three days and canceled their basketball games. The event, called a "lockout," caused community members and the players' parents to get quite upset, catching the media's attention, which eventually led to the making of the movie.

As soon as kids make it on to their high school teams, they often start looking for a college scholarship. Many parents push their kids to get an athletic scholarship to pay for college. In a survey of high school football and basketball players, 59 percent believed they would receive a college scholarship, but only 1 to 2 percent actually do, according to Mike Blackburn of the Interscholastic Athletic

Administration.

Kids also dream of "hitting it big" or becoming professional athletes and making lots of money. They see what basketball star Lebron James did. While still in high school, James signed an endorsement contract with Nike worth between $90 million and $100 million dollars. So did Kobe Bryant, who passed up college to join the Los Angeles Lakers. No wonder high school kids look at the playing field and see green dollar bills growing from the ground instead of grass. The dream to be a professional athlete is just as strong as the wish for a scholarship to college.

Northeastern University's Center for the Study of Sports in Society surveyed American young people and found that one-third of young African-American boys, ages 13 to 18, believed that they could earn a living playing professional sports. This belief in sports as a ticket to the future was more than double that of Caucasian boys in the same age group. For African-American males, playing sports is often seen as a chance for economic mobility. Though African-Americans make up 13 percent of the U.S. population, they make up the majority of players in two of our professional sports: 76 percent of pro basketball players and 66 percent of pro football players. African Americans also make up 22 percent of pro soccer players, according to the Institute for Diversity and Ethics in Sport, which tracks race and gender in the professional leagues.

Yet the odds of making it through all the steps from high school to the NBA or NFL are slim. High school students get recruited for college teams. From college teams, only the best players get drafted into the pro leagues. The National Collegiate Interscholastic Association tracks the number of high school players who have gone into the pro leagues over the years and have calculated the odds: 3 out of 10,000 high school basketball players will play for the NBA. For high school football players, the odds are that approximately 1 in 1,000 will be drafted into the NFL.

Sports in College – The Student-Athlete

When athletes go to college on a scholarship, they are often quickly hit with the harsh financial and cultural realities of playing in college. According to the National Collegiate Athletic Association, the average athletic scholarship is $8,707 per year, which is nowhere near the price of full college tuition. In sports like baseball or track and field, the figure is routinely as low as $2,000. Tuition and room and board for college often cost between $20,000 and $50,000 a year.

There is a lot of pressure to be what we call the *student-athlete,* or the high school or college student who gets both a high grade-point average and plays very well on a sports team. In college, especially, it's extremely hard to do both activities well as there is more emphasis on winning a college game than on maintaining good grades. In fact, the graduation rate from college for athletes playing on their college team is relatively low. College athletes, unlike professionals, do not earn salaries, but they have demanding hours for practices and training sessions. There might be an early morning weight-lifting session, various team meetings, and long trips to games. Their commitment to the team may limit the courses they can take, so they take classes for credit, but not to earn a degree.

College athletes might feel they don't fit into the rest of the student body, which often views them as privileged. As a result of the demanding schedule and the alienation, some first- and second-year athletes are forced to give up their athletic scholarships. Estimates vary on how many student athletes graduate in five years, as it depends on the sport, but the graduation rates for college student athletes range from 53 to 72 percent, the Institute for Diversity and Ethics in Sport reports, which tracks graduation success rates. The NCAA, which regulates college sports, has toughened the academic standards for college student athletes in recent years. It has become stricter about athletes maintaining a certain grade-point average in order to continue playing on the college team.

As a result of this new trend, universities are trying hard to improve graduation rates by building tutoring centers just for their student athletes. The academic centers include services such as one-on-one tutoring from other undergraduates, career counseling, therapy for learning disabilities, and staff to see that athletes get to class. *The Chronicle of Higher Education* reported in 2008 that universities with strong sports programs have more than doubled their spending on tutoring athletes over the past decade. These centers are usually run by the athletic department of the college and have been used as a recruiting device for coaches.

A few universities that have recently built million-dollar academic centers strictly for student athletes include the University of Michigan in Ann Arbor, Duke University, Louisiana State University, Texas A&M University, and the University of Illinois. The University of Oregon is also building an athletic facility, which is being paid for by Philip H. Knight, the billionaire founder of Nike. Supporters of these athletic complexes argue that the price tag for the tutoring centers is relatively small in comparison to the money made by university athletic events. For example, the University of Michigan's 2008 expected budget for athletic events is $87 million in revenues, while its athletic-tutoring center would cost $1 million. As we can see, college sports is big business in the United States.

Working Hard at Leisure

When American players are interviewed by a sports reporter after a game, they are often asked to comment about their win or loss. American players usually say something like this: "We had a job to do. We got the job done." As if the game was a job. It's all right because they had to work hard to achieve the win. Why, it's the old value of hard work mixed with the new resource of leisure time. It may be said that it's a winning combination.

Notes

"I always turn to the sports section first. The sports page records people's accomplishments; the front page has nothing but man's failures."

--Earl Warren, Chief Justice, U. S. Supreme Court
(1891-1974)

Bibliography

Abramson, John. *Overdosed America: The Broken Promise of American Medicine*. New York: Harper Collins, September 2004.

Ackermann, Marsha. *Cool Comfort: America's Romance with Air Conditioning*. Washington D.C.: Smithsonian Institution Press, 2002.

Bennett, Lerone Jr. *Before the Mayflower: A History of Black America*. New York:Penguin, 1984.

Blackburn, Mike. "The Purpose of High School Athletics is Not for the Development of Professional Athletes." *Interscholastic Athletic Administration*, Volume #31, Number 1, Fall 2004.

Branch, John. "Promising Fans In Seats a View From the Couch." *The New York Times,* January 29, 2009.

Bureau of Justice. *Homicide Trends in the United States*, Washington, D.C., 2000.

Davies, Richard O. *America's Obsession: Sports and Society Since 1945*. Independence, Kentucky: Wadsworth Publishing, 1994

Chakravorti, Sujit, and Timothy McHugh. "Why do we use so many checks?" *Economic Perspectives Report*, Federal Reserve Bank of Chicago, 2002.

Gallup Annual Lifestyle Poll. "What Is Your Favorite Sport to Watch?" December 2008.

The Harris Poll, #77. "Firefighters, Scientists and Teachers Top List as "Most Prestigious Occupations," August 1, 2007.

Interagency Council on the Homeless. *Homelessness: Programs and the People They Serve*, U.S. Bureau of the Census, 1999.

Jacobs, Lawrence R. "1994 All Over Again? Public Opinion and Health Care." *The New England Journal of Medicine*, Volume 358.18, May 1, 2008.

Jones, Grahame, "Mexico's team feels at home in the U.S." *Los Angeles Times*, February 6, 2008.

Keckley, Paul H. and Underwood, Howard R. "Medical Tourism: Consumers in Search of Value." *Deloitte Center for Health Solutions*, 2008.

Killias, Martin, John van Kesteren, and Martin Rindlisbacher. "Guns, violent crime and suicide in 21 countries." in *Canadian Journal of Criminology*, vol. 43/4, October 2002.

Klein, Jim and Martha Olsen. "How GM Destroyed the U.S. Rail System." *Auto Free Times*, vol. 10, January 30, 1999.

Kosmin, Barry A. and Seymour P. Lachman. *One Nation Under God*. New York: Harmony Books, 1993.

Kosmin, Barry A. and Egon Mayer. *American Religious Identification Survey*, New York: City University of New York, 2001.

Lederer, Richard. *The Miracle of English*. New York: Pocket Books, 1991.

Mandelbaum, Michael. *The Meaning of Sports*. New York: Public Affairs, 2004.

Mayer, Don. "Institutionalizing Overconsumption: The Oil Industry and Destruction of Public Transport." in *The Business of Consumption*, eds. Laura Westra and Patricia H. Werhane, June 1998.

McCrum, Robert, William Cran, and Robert MacNeil. *The Story of English*. New York: Viking Penguin Press, 1986.

Menzel, Peter. *Material World*. New York: Random House, 1993.

National Center for Educational Statistics. "Pursuing Excellence: A Study of U.S. Twelfth-Grade Mathematics and Science Achievement in International Context." *Third International Mathematics and Science Study*, Washington D.C., 1998.

National Center for Health Statistics. "An Overview of Nursing Home Facilities." *National Nursing Home Survey*, Advance Data No. 311, March 1, 2000.

National Geographic Society. *Global Geographic Literacy Survey*, National Geographic-Roper, 2002.

Nolte, Ellen and McKee, Martin C. "Measuring the Health of Nations: Updating an Earlier Analysis," *Health Affairs*, January/February 2008.

Organization for Economic Co-operation and Development (OECD). "Pharmaceutical Pricing Policy Project." October 27, 2008.

Pennington, Bill. "Expectations Lose to Reality of Sports Scholarships." *The New York Times*, March 10, 2008.

Pitman, Joanna. *On Blondes*. New York: Bloomsbury, 2003.

Pucher, John and Lewis Dijkstra. "Making Walking and Cycling Safer: Lessons from Europe," in *Transportation Quarterly*, Vol. 54, No. 3, Summer 2000.

Schoen, Cathy et al. "Taking the Pulse of Health Care Systems: Experiences of Patients with Health Problems in Six Countries." *Health Affairs*, Vol. 16, November 3, 2005.

Schoen, Cathy et al., "Primary Care and Health System Performance: Adults' Experiences in Five Countries," *Health Affairs*, Web Exclusive , October 28, 2004.

Stremikis, Kristof, et all. "Health Care Opinion Leaders Survey." *Commonwealth Fund/Modern Healthcare*, November 2008.

The U.S. Census Bureau. *Income, Poverty, and Health Insurance Coverage in the United States: 2007*, August 2008.

Weightman, Gavin. *The Frozen-Water Trade: A True Story*. New York: Hyperion, 2003.

Wolverton, Brad. "Spending Plenty So Athletes Can Make the Grade." *The Chronicle of Higher Education*, September 5, 2008.

Woolhandler, Steffie M.D. et al. "Costs of Health Care Administration in the United States and Canada." *The New England Journal of Medicine*, Volume 349: 768-775. August 21, 2003.

World Health Organization. *The World Health Report 2000 – Health systems: Improving Performance*. Geneva: June 21, 2000. (http://www.who.int/whr/2008).

Zoss, Joel and Bowen, John. *Diamonds in the Rough: The Untold Story of Baseball*. New York: McGraw-Hill/Contemporary, 1996.

Selected Websites

American Civil Liberties Union. Reports on the number of prisoners in the United States. (www.aclu.org)

American Discovery Trail. Information on the coast-to-coast trail. (www.discoverytrail.org)

American Educational Statistics (www.nces.ed.gov)

Amnesty International. Reports on executions by country. (www. amnesty.org)

Animal Legal Defense Fund. (www.aldf.org)

Bureau of Justice. Reports on crime, victims and homicide trends in the U.S. (www.ojp.usdoj.gov/bjs/cvict.htm)

Chivalry. (www.chivalrytoday.com)

The Commonwealth Fund. A private foundation that tracks trends in health coverage, access and quality. (www.cmwf. org)

The Death Penalty Information Center. Statistics on the death penalty. (www.deathpenaltyinfo.org)

Divorce Reform. (www.divorcereform.org)

Federal Bureau of Investigation. The Uniform Crime Reports Program collects crime data in the United States, including the number of hate crimes. (www.fbi.gov/ucr)

Frivolous lawsuits. (www.power-of-attorneys.com)

The Institute for Diversity and Ethics in Sport (TIDES) at the University of Central Florida. Issues an annual "Race and Gender Report Card" on sports. (www.bus.ucf.edu)

Selected Websites

The Kaiser Family Foundation. This is a non-profit private operating foundation that doesresearch and analysis on health issues. (kff.org)

National Collegiate Association, 2005 Study on Athletic Scholarships. (www.ncaa.org)

The National Collegiate Athletic Association. Reports on the number of college athletic scholarships awarded to high school athletes. (www.ncaa.org)

National League of Cities. Reports on curfews in the U.S. (www.nlc.org.)

National Center for Health Statistics. Statistics on health for the United States. (www.cdc.gov/nchs)

Northeastern University's Center for the Study of Sport in Society. Reports on problems in sports and shows how sports can help benefit society. (sportsinsociety.org)

The New England Journal of Medicine. A respected medical journal. (www.nejm.org)

National Center of Aging. (www.ncoa.org)

U.S. Census Bureau. Population and demographic data. (www.census.gov)

Women's Sports Federation. Reports on the number of female athletes in the U.S. (www.womenssportsfoundation.org)

World Health Organization. An agency of the United Nation that reports on international public health issues. (www.who.org)

Index

About the Author

During the wee hours of one snowy day in January, the author became a citizen of East Detroit, a small suburb where people live on square subdivision plots, hemmed in by the fear of going too far south and reaching downtown Detroit, or too far east and falling in the Great Lakes of Michigan.

There she was raised, received her college education, and trained in the way a good wholesome girl from the Midwest should go. She didn't go that way. First, she majored in international relations, and then she had to see those faraway places with strange-sounding names.

Her passion for cultures other than her own led her to Mexico where she worked as a reporter while trying to master the subjunctive tense and all the names for hot peppers. In New York City, she freelanced for newspapers and magazines, counseled Vietnamese refugees, copyedited books for lawyers, and interpreted in the local courts.

She now lives in San Diego with her Ecuadorian husband, Angel, who lets her speak Spanish with a fierce American accent, and her daughter, Sonia. She teaches English to international students at the University of California – San Diego. As a speaker, teacher and intercultural trainer, she has helped countless international newcomers feel at home in the United States.